Y0-BWY-189

GRACE
ALL
THE WAY
HOME

GRACE ALL THE WAY HOME

A Study of Romans

Mark Trotter

THE UPPER ROOM
Nashville, Tennessee

Grace All the Way Home

Copyright © 1982 The Upper Room. All rights reserved. No part of this book may be reproduced in any manner whatsoever without permission of the publisher except in brief quotations embodied in critical articles or reviews. For information address The Upper Room, 1908 Grand Avenue, P. O. Box 189, Nashville, Tennessee 37202.

Scripture quotations not otherwise identified are from the Revised Standard Version of the Bible, copyrighted 1946, 1952, and © 1971 by the Division of Christian Education, National Council of Churches of Christ in the United States of America, and are used by permission.

Quotations designated KJV are from the King James Version of the Bible.

Quotations designated TLB are from *The Living Bible,* copyright © 1971 by Tyndale House Publishers.

Dag Hammarskjöld's prayer is reprinted from *Markings* by Dag Hammarskjöld, translated by Leif Sjöberg and W. H. Auden and copyright © 1964 by Alfred A. Knopf, Inc., and Faber and Faber, Ltd., and is used with the permission of the publisher, Alfred A. Knopf, Inc.

The poem "John Brown's Body" by Stephen Vincent Benet is from *The Selected Works of Stephen Vincent Benet,* published by Holt, Rinehart & Winston, Inc. Copyright renewed 1955, 1956 by Rosemary Carr Benet, and is reprinted by permission of Brandt & Brandt Literary Agents, Inc.

Book Design: Linda Bryant
First printing: January, 1982 (10)
Library of Congress Catalog Card Number: 81–52860
ISBN: 0 – 8358 – 0434 – 8

Printed in the United States of America

Contents

CONTENTS

Foreword

In the early sixties, my brother Irwin and I made a pilgrimage to hear the great Swiss theologian Karl Barth. He was visiting America for the first time, and, as it turned out, the last time, and we felt compelled to drive to San Francisco to hear him speak. The seminary president who introduced him described Barth as "a glacier who has carved out the valley in which all of us now live."

In retrospect the metaphor seems a bit grand though it sounded appropriate at the time. A lot has happened in the last twenty years, and the excitement caused by Barth's provocative writings has ebbed. Barth was awakened to the meaning of the gospel for the European culture between the world wars by reading Paul's Letter to the Romans. Before Barth, Wesley was reborn through hearing the reading of Luther's commentary on Romans. Luther had received the insight that freed his soul and fired the Protestant Reformation from his own encounter with Romans. Before Luther, Augustine was called to his vocation by confronting the same letter.

So it is really Paul who is the glacier. His Letter to the Romans has shaped not only Christianity but the western world as has no other document. Its phrases are the stuff out of which reformations and revolutions are formed. Augustine, Luther, Wesley,

Barth were only four world shakers out of many who were inspired by this small letter.

It was with that consciousness that I accepted the challenge to write a reflection on Romans. I am not a biblical scholar or a professional theologian, but a journeyman pastor who seeks to make the biblical message come alive to those who live twenty centuries after Paul wrote the church in Rome.

I am indebted to the congregation of the First United Methodist Church in San Diego, who have heard some of this material in one form or another and responded helpfully, and especially to Margaret Fulcomer, my secretary, who typed the manuscript.

Introduction

There are several approaches to bible study. The most common is the devotional style, reading the scripture without aids or commentaries and allowing the text to speak to you in the most literal way. Though often successful as a catalyst for sharing personal experiences in small groups, the shortcoming of this approach is that the most obvious meaning of a passage may not be the most accurate.

To uncover what the text originally said, the historical-critical approach is needed. Many individuals or groups prefer this style which uses commentaries and bible dictionaries to aid them in recreating the original historical setting for the text. In this approach the question, "What does the text really say?" is asked before the question, "What does it mean for my life?"

A third approach is to take the major themes of a biblical text, use scholarly tools to discover the original message, examine them in light of traditional doctrines, and finally illustrate how the teaching illumines our lives. I suppose this could be called a "doctrinal" or "topical" style. This book is based on such a style.

In the United Methodist tradition, the individual Christian is called to do theology, to do his or her own thinking about the meaning of the Christian faith. I would hope this book will serve as an aid to that important task. It is not the definitive work on Paul, but one believer's understanding, offered to encourage others to do their own theology. It can be used in groups as a commentary along with more scholarly tools. Or it can be used with individual devotions, a way of examining your life in light of Paul's understanding of the meaning of Jesus Christ for the world.

I

Justification
by Faith
in God's Grace

But now the righteousness of God has been manifested apart from law, although the law and the prophets bear witness to it, the righteousness of God through faith in Jesus Christ for all who believe. For there is no distinction; since all have sinned and fall short of the glory of God, they are justified by his grace as a gift, through the redemption which is in Christ Jesus, whom God put forward as an expiation by his blood, to be received by faith.

This was to show God's righteousness, because in his divine forbearance he had passed over former sins; it was to prove at the present time that he himself is righteous and that he justifies him who has faith in Jesus.

—Romans 3:21–26

Main Show

ring back good memories of the
.owns, and wild animal acts. But
ig top is gone and the circus is
. Even the sideshows and carnival
orbidden delights and the promise
of the strange ᴀ.._ ᴠe disappeared.
Allen Wheelis is a practicing psychoanalyst in San Francisco
and also writes books. In *On Not Knowing How to Live*, he talked
about developing a philosophy of life, using the big top as an
analogy:

> Stay with the main show, do not be drawn off into side shows, diver-
> sions, entertainments. Do only what you are most solemnly charged to
> do. . . . There in the big top a man is hanging by his teeth, twisting,
> spinning, spotlights playing over him, the drums beginning to roll.
> He's going to fall and nothing can be done, no net, but in the moments
> remaining he may yet achieve something remarkable, some glittering
> stunt, a movement perhaps of breathtaking beauty. . . . Any turning
> away to watch the dancing bears is a betrayal of the dangling man. . . .
> Hold fast, stay with him.

Wheelis's advice can be adapted to the Christian faith. There
are religious sideshows being offered with enticing attractions and

claims to fabulous feats of supernatural power and miraculous cures, things you just wouldn't believe—the religious versions of dancing bears, stripteases, and peep shows. These are the sideshows. They come and they go.

And then there is the main show. The main show features not an aerialist now, but a man on a cross. Stay with him. Focus on the meaning of what he is doing for your life. Do not be drawn into the sideshows of religion, the diversions and the entertainments. Any turning away from his sacrifice is a betrayal of the man on the cross. If you want to make the most of the time given you, before the tent comes down, stay with the main show. Stay with the man on the cross.

Paul sent similar advice to the church at Rome. From the beginning, Christians have been tempted to the sideshows, to those preachers who claim all kinds of things for the Christian faith—from material prosperity to spiritual ecstasy. Just step right up. Buy a ticket and all this will be yours.

To the hawkers of all these sideshows, the cross was an embarrassment. They didn't know what to do with it. They felt the cross was something they had to explain. Paul says it is something we are given to proclaim. The cross is the main show. Everything else is a sideshow.

Paul's individual contribution to the church was to sort out the significant from the trivial. Whenever the church has been diverted to a sideshow, some religious fad, Paul is rediscovered and we are called back to the main show. Most of the time this passage from Romans sparked the reform.

There is no distinction; since all have sinned and fall short of the glory of God, they are justified by his grace as a gift, through the redemption which is in Christ Jesus.

—Romans 3:22–24

If someone were to ask you what the goal of your life is, what it is that you want out of life, you would probably answer, "To be fulfilled as a person," or, "To know success in my life," or, "To have peace of mind."

STAY WITH THE MAIN SHOW

If Paul had been asked the same question, he would have answered unhesitatingly, "Righteousness." Neither Paul nor any other serious Jew of the first century would have given it a second thought. The goal of life had been clearly enunciated: Be righteous. And the way to righteousness had been plainly revealed by God in what they called "the Law."

One day, they believed, everybody will stand before God and be judged according to the Law. And that meant everybody. If you protested that you are not Jewish, and that you don't even know what the Law is, Paul would have said that doesn't matter. "You have no excuse. The Jews received the Law written on stone, but you have it written on your hearts" (Rom. 2:15, author's paraphrase). Therefore no one is exempt. Everybody must stand before God and be judged by the Law and if you measure up God will declare you to be "righteous." To be deemed "righteous" in the sight of God was to be justified.

The goal of Paul's life was to have God say, "Paul, you are justified. You did a good job. You lived a righteous life."

When Paul got the point of what God was doing in Jesus Christ, he said the good news is that we are justified not by our works but by God's grace. Paul analyzed our situation in this way: We will never measure up. To try to earn our own salvation is to ask for failure. If we try to be righteous by our own efforts, we only succeed in being self-righteous. If we live our lives trying to be perfect in all things, we end up feeling like failures in everything. If we believe we have to earn our worth through good deeds, our deeds will always be self-serving. All efforts to justify our own existence fall short.

The good news is that God has justified us by grace as a gift. It is as if the judgment has already taken place on the cross, so you can stop running around trying to justify your existence. "I accept you," God proclaims, "so stop trying to make yourself acceptable to others. Stop punishing yourself for not being perfect." The message of the cross is that God has taken the punishment which, in reality, should be ours.

Paul wanted to know, "Is my life justified?" He looked at the cross and knew the answer was yes.

John Wesley worked as hard as Paul to achieve what he called "assurance." He believed all the doctrines of the Christian faith obediently. He believed everything but that was not enough. What he believed in his head didn't make any difference in his life. He experienced the same kind of discouragement you and I feel when we sense that the faith we hold promises more than it has ever delivered to us. If we are saved, how come we don't feel that way? If we are redeemed, why don't we celebrate our lives more? That was Wesley's question.

His answer was to be more religious, to try harder to obey the rules, to the end that he became less Christian. In Georgia, serving as priest to the colonists, he did things he wished he hadn't done. He couldn't admit it, but he had misused his office and had hurt people. As a result he was fired from his job.

Returning to England, he visited his brother Charles, sick in bed with pleurisy. Charles confided to John that in the crisis of the illness, when his life was in peril, he had experienced the assurance of God's love and felt that no matter what happened, now he was going to be all right. He was able to accept each day as a gift from God and enjoy it.

John had never been able to live that way. He felt he had struggled for the assurance of God's love harder than anyone else in England. When he saw that Charles had received, apparently with no effort, what he had worked for so hard and was denied, he experienced the most profound discouragement.

In that despondent mood on May 24, 1738, he went to Aldersgate to a meeting of the Moravians. Wesley had first observed these German immigrants on board ship when sailing to the Georgia colony. A storm had battered the ship to the point that even the veteran seamen had panicked. Everybody was terrified except the Moravians, who gathered together, prayed, and sang hymns. Apparently they were oblivious to the storm, as if the peace inside them had calmed the storm outside. Wesley learned they called that inner peace "assurance."

And he knew he didn't have it, as many of us know we don't have it. It enables you to accept whatever happens to you, trusting that it is going to be all right, to ride out the storms of life knowing that Jesus is Lord even over the storms. It enables you to say, "I don't need to be in control of all things, nor of every moment of my life, because I know who is in control."

I don't think this could ever be proved, but I am sure that the first verse of Charles Wesley's hymn "Jesus, Lover of My Soul" was inspired by John's remembrance of the Moravians on board ship in the Atlantic.

> Jesus, lover of my soul,
> Let me to thy bosom fly,
> While the nearer waters roll,
> While the tempest still is high:
> Hide me, O my Savior, hide,
> Till the storm of life is past;
> Safe into the haven guide;
> O receive my soul at last!

That's what he wanted: Assurance!

So on that night in 1738, as was his custom, he went to Evensong at St. Paul's Cathedral and heard the choir sing the *"De Profundis"* (Out of the Depths, I Cry to Thee"), echoing his own despair. Then, he went reluctantly to Aldersgate Street, to the meeting of the Moravians. He sat quietly as the leader read from Luther's "Preface to Paul's Letter to the Romans," where Luther talks about being justified by God's grace as a gift and not by our own works. Wesley had heard that a thousand times. He had even preached it. But that night he finally understood it. He described what happened:

> I felt my heart strangely warmed. I felt I did trust in Christ, Christ alone, for salvation; and an assurance was given me, that He had taken away my sins, even mine, and saved me from the law of sin and death.

If you asked Paul what was the goal of his life, he would say, "Justification." If you asked Wesley, he would answer, "Assurance." And if you asked Ken Olson, he would say, "Self-esteem."

Ken Olson tried always to be perfect. He had to be successful. He could never afford to fail because of what failure would mean to his self-esteem. Later he realized that his fear of failure was essentially a religious problem. He came to see that he was living under the Law and not by grace. He had enough religion to worry about how he was doing, but not enough to enjoy what he was doing.

In his book *The Art of Hanging Loose in an Uptight World,* Olson gave an illustration of his problem. He grew up in Phoenix and played high school football under the legendary Walt Ruth. Olson called Ruth "the Vince Lombardi of high school football." Ruth demanded 100 percent cooperation and dedication from all his players. He made them work hard. He was tremendously successful as a coach and would not tolerate failure. If you sat down during practice or drank water, you ran laps. If you fumbled, you ran laps. When Walt Ruth said, "Jump," the team shouted back, "How high?"

Olson played defensive halfback. In one of the first games in his senior year, the end on the opposition team managed to get behind him to catch the pass for a touchdown that won the game. Olson was humiliated.

But it got worse. The next day his picture was on the front page of the newspaper, arms outstretched trying to block the pass, the football falling into the arms of the receiver for the touchdown. Now if you are a person who doesn't like to let other people know you make mistakes, your error being illustrated on the front page of the newspaper can be devastating.

Then the thing he feared most happened. On Monday morning, when he arrived at school, he was told Ruth was waiting to see him. When Olson entered the office, he saw the picture from the newspaper on the coach's desk. The man Olson looked up to was about to confront him with his failure. "What do you have to say about this picture?" the coach asked. Predictably Olson replied, "I'm sorry; I'll try harder." Ruth said, "Look at the picture again, closely this time. Look at your face. Look at your muscles. Can't you see that's your problem? You're trying too hard. Now, I want you to relax. I want you to believe in yourself. You are going to be a great player.''

We all live under some law, although we give it different names. The law is that which says do this or that, and if we don't do it very well, we punish ourselves by eating too much, drinking too much, failing at things we should have no difficulty with, blaming other people for our condition. Living under the law means we will always be running laps for a demanding coach.

Paul, Wesley, and Olson had that in common. They all lived under a law. But they had one more thing in common. They all came to live by grace. They all made their way, finally, to the ''big top'' and saw the man on the cross and heard the news: The judgment already has taken place! You are justified by grace as a gift through the redemption of Christ Jesus.

They received by grace the gifts they could never earn by their own efforts: justification, assurance of God's love, and self-esteem.

II

From Adam
to Christ

For the wrath of God is revealed from heaven against all ungodliness and wickedness of men who by their wickedness suppress the truth. For what can be known about God is plain to them, because God has shown it to them. Ever since the creation of the world his invisible nature, namely, his eternal power and deity, has been clearly preceived in the things that have been made. So they are without excuse; for although they knew God they did not honor him as God or give thanks to him, but they became futile in their thinking and their senseless minds were darkened. Claiming to be wise, they became fools, and exchanged the glory of the immortal God for images resembling mortal man or birds or animals or reptiles.

—Romans 1:18–23

So I find it to be a law that when I want to do right, evil lies close at hand. For I delight in the law of God, in my inmost self, but I see in my members another law at war with the law of my mind and making me captive to the law of sin which dwells in my members. Wretched man that I am! Who will deliver me from this body of death? Thanks be to God through Jesus Christ our Lord! So then, I of myself serve the law of God with my mind, but with my flesh I serve the law of sin.

—Romans 7:21–25

2

Dr. Jekyll and Mr. Hyde

The main show is the man on the cross, and its theme is, ''You are justified by God's grace alone.'' Paul gets downright lyrical whenever he writes about grace. Some of the most inspired prose ever written comes from his description of what grace means for human life. That's the main show, and Paul is never distracted from it.

But Paul doesn't start there. He ends up in theology but he starts out in psychology. He ends with God's grace but he begins with our sin. In the first two chapters of Romans, and then again in the seventh, he sets out to answer the questions, Why do we need grace in the first place? Why can't we make it by ourselves? His diagnosis sounds like depth psychology.

Now if I do what I do not want, it is no longer I that do it, but sin which dwells within me. So I find it to be a law that when I want to do right, evil lies close at hand.

—Romans 7:20–21

The first time I heard the story of Dr. Jekyll and Mr. Hyde it scared me. But because I was raised in a rational and orderly environment that taught me that human life is essentially good, I looked upon Jekyll and Hyde as merely a story, an early example of science fiction. It was not until I grew older that I got the point that *The Strange Case of Dr. Jekyll and Mr. Hyde* is not merely fantasy. It is a diagnosis of the human condition.

There is an intriguing irony in the title. Dr. Jekyll, the respectable scientist, has a name that sounds like "jackal," the wild dog that stalks at night for its prey. Mr. Hyde implies that he is hidden. Robert Louis Stevenson must have chosen the names intentionally to make the point that within the civilized, rational person is a hidden beast.

The novel was written in 1888. In that most optimistic age that produced an amazing number of utopian novels, Stevenson's story stands almost alone as a dissenting voice. It was a warning to the properly mannered, well-educated, and morally upright person, that there lies in that person a primitive, violent brute. The power of science, symbolized by the potion Dr. Jekyll concocts in his laboratory, can just as easily release the beast in human life as create a paradise on earth, a warning our century has vindicated.

It is hard for those of us living in the latter part of the twentieth century to recapture the optimism that existed at the end of the nineteenth century. Awesome technological achievement and scientific advance generated a vibrant humanitarianism, heralding a new day. The "progress" civilized people made was remarkable. That pernicious institution, the slave trade that had plagued humankind for thousands of years, was finally outlawed in the English-speaking world. Reforms were instituted in treating people with mental disorders. Hospitals became places where people would go to get well and not just to die. The settlement house movement had begun in the cities of America, promising concern for the poor. The International Red Cross was created. The YMCA was organized. The missionary enterprise, one of the most optimistic of all the enterprises of the church, was cresting and promising to bring the whole world to Christ in one generation. And the Olympic games were revived to show that polite competition could take place between people of all nations, free from the influence of politics and selfish gain.

A gentle, Christian humanism pervaded the end of the

nineteenth century, and the world expectantly prepared for the twentieth, confident that they were about to enter into a new millenium of peace and goodwill. One religious journal, founded two years before Stevenson wrote *The Strange Case of Dr. Jekyll and Mr. Hyde,* shared the optimism of that era and in 1900 renamed itself *The Christian Century.*

And then it hit: 1914, and, as Lord Grey put it, "The lamps are going out all over Europe." It was as if Mr. Hyde, the bestial part of human nature lying beneath the respectable, had escaped. In four years the great European civilization was in ruin, and in the rubble lay the dream of a Christian century.

Then in succession, there occurred the Russian Revolution, the Great Depression, the rise of Hitler, the Spanish Civil War, World War II, the Korean War, the Vietnam War. With each decade of this century the capacity for destruction and evil has increased and the possibilities for building a world of peace have decreased. Today we have opportunity for achieving good in the world, perhaps greater than before. But we have also come to the terrible realization that there is even greater probability of destruction.

We will never be the same again. We have seen too much. We have seen that in Dr. Jekyll—that respectable, civilized, educated, religious, moral man—there lies a Mr. Hyde. How do you explain that? Humankind marching triumphantly toward unprecedented heights of grandeur and then, without reason, descending into unparalleled inhumanity?

During World War I, Karl Barth was the pastor of a village church in Switzerland. The lights *had* gone out in Europe. His people were crying for some word that would make sense out of what had happened. Barth, who had been raised in the nineteenth century and trained in its optimistic humanism, found that he had nothing to preach. He turned to the scriptures in desperation and discovered what he called, in *The Word of God and the Word of Man,* "the strange new world within the Bible." It was strange because it described a world unlike the image of the world held by the confident liberals of the nineteenth century. And when he came to Paul's Letter to the Romans, he found there a diagnosis of human nature that offered a reason for the chaos of his time.

Paul begins with a realism about sin. He rejects the idea that sin is something we can get rid of with proper upbringing, healthy environments, evolutionary development, great civilization, or even religious conversion. Sin lies beneath the surface of all our lives, like Mr. Hyde. Don't be naïve, Paul says, about the dimension of sin in your life. Don't dismiss Mr. Hyde as fantasy.

Surveying the ruins of a house in a badly-blitzed town in the west of England during the war, an English preacher remarked to the owner, a lady of fine character, that this was original sin in operation. She turned to him with a look of pained surprise and said, "But surely you don't believe in that dreadful doctrine?" To which he replied, "Such dreadful happenings as these," pointing to the ruins, "demand some sort of dreadful doctrine in explanation."

Paul won't let you be naïve about sin. But if you do not read him carefully, you may come away pessimistic about human possibility—and to reach that conclusion from Paul is to misread him. As we will see, some of the most triumphant prose written about human life came from Paul. But in these passages he is overstating his case to make a point. He is a convert and he is expressing the enthusiasm of all converts.

Some young people came to visit me. They had been members of the church but had left to join a sectarian group. They returned now as missionaries with the intentions of converting me to their faith. They were like hunters seeking a prized trophy. They wanted to bring back a real live Methodist *clericus giganticus,* but I managed to escape them through the jungle of theological obfuscation. Their tactic was to describe my condition as absolute darkness, total ignorance, and an unmitigated error. I thought I was just a run-of-the-mill, wishy-washy United Methodist, but they saw me as desperately lost, heading for hell and damnation.

The temptation of all converts is to describe the world in absolute terms: light and darkness, good and evil, saved and damned. There is some of that simplistic view of the world in Paul. He has the enthusiasm of the convert who views those who have not had his experience as lost.

In addition, there is the preacher in Paul that wants to persuade. His purpose is to impress upon the Romans that the news that God has come to us in Jesus Christ was totally unexpected and undeserved. Paul couldn't get over the fact that we didn't find God, God found us. We didn't earn God's love, it was given freely.

To make that point as strongly as possible, Paul and most of his interpreters insist that there is no virtue in us that compelled that love. There is no merit in us that earned God's grace. It was undeserved, unmerited grace "that saved a wretch like me."

That kind of language is called *hyperbole*. Its purpose is to make a point as strongly as possible. It is not the language of science. It is the language of persuasion. Paul was no wretch and he knew it. He was a good man. In other letters he will even boast of his goodness. And if we apply our own experience, our reason, and the tradition of other Christian teaching—including Paul's own letters, not to mention the teaching of Jesus—we will have to qualify Paul's rhetoric. We are not totally lost, none of us. We are created by God in God's image. We are created good, and we never lose that essential goodness. Human beings are not wretches.

So Paul uses hyperbole to insist that God's love for us is unmerited. Once we sort that out we can learn from his diagnosis that underneath all human achievement a force threatens to corrupt all good works. Paul is saying we already know when we are honest. Beneath the surface, behind the facade of righteousness or religiosity or morality or success or happiness, a war is going on between our real feelings and our surface appearances—between our regrets and our dreams, between our desires and our conscience. These desires, regrets, and feelings, if they were ever set loose, would probably embarrass us—even shame us—and, more times than we like to admit, they control our behavior.

When Paul wrote, "I do not do the good I want but the evil I do not want is what I end up doing," it was not the confession of an evil man. It was the honesty of a good man, a man who wanted to do what was right, but who discovered that there was another force at work in him. He describes that force as a conflict between flesh and spirit. In *Pensées,* Blaise Pascal described it as a struggle between grandeur and misery. Carl Sandburg contrasted an eagle which soars into the heights with a hog which wallows in the mud. Stevenson described it as a struggle between Dr. Jekyll and Mr. Hyde.

There is a war going on, and Paul won't let us be naïve about it, or let us think that we can easily resolve it. We won't. It may not make wretches out of us, but it will probably make us self-righteous. It may not turn us into monsters, just egotists. We won't be guilty of murder, but we can easily assassinate another person's character. We would never treat someone unjustly, but we will live complacently in a society that passes laws that treat other people unjustly. We would never rob someone and leave him or her on the side of the road to die, but we will prosper with good conscience in a world that exploits the poor. We may want to do the good, but sometimes, in spite of ourselves, we end up doing the very thing we don't want to do.

I know I am that way. I have wanted to do the right thing, but I lacked the courage. I wanted to do the humble thing, but I was too proud. I wanted to do the loving thing, but I was afraid to make myself vulnerable. I wanted to think of other people and their needs, but I couldn't stop thinking of myself.

Many therapies are offered that enable us to live with our divided selves. Some say that it is all right to be the way we are, no matter what the way we are happens to be. After reading some books, I feel very good about myself. And if I compare myself to a selected sample of other people, I have the same good feeling. But when I compare myself to what I know God wants me to be, I realize that I have fallen short, and I know that if my salvation depends on my making myself be what God wants me to be, then I will never do it; I will always fall short.

That is precisely what Paul was led to see when he stumbled on the Christian gospel. Søren Kierkegaard says that from the world's point of view, when we become aware of the duplicity of our motives, we are the most to be pitied. But from the Christian point of view, at that moment of self-awareness, we are the most to be envied, because at that moment we are ready at last to understand the Good News.

Fifteen hundred years after Paul, Martin Luther reached that point in life in which the world pitied him. After years of trying to gain salvation by living an exemplary life, he plummeted into what he called *Anfechtung*. It is translated "temptation," but we would recognize it as depression. As therapy, a wise counselor in the monastery assigned him to the new university at Wittenberg to teach Paul's letters. And so Luther, with eyes ready to see and with a mind ready to understand and with a heart ready to believe, turned to the Letter to the Romans. When he read, "I do not do the good I want, but the evil I do not want is what I do," he knew that Paul was talking about him. And when he read, "Since all have sinned and fall short of the glory of God, they are justified by . . . grace as a gift" (Rom. 3:23–24), he knew that God had touched his life, even his.

Having experienced that grace, Luther could write these words in his hymn "A Mighty Fortress Is Our God":

> Did we in our own strength confide,
> Our striving would be losing,
> Were not the right Man on our side,
> The Man of God's own choosing:
> Dost ask who that may be?
> Christ Jesus, it is He;
> Lord Sabaoth is His name,
> From age to age the same,
> And He must win the battle.

That same battle rages in you and me.

While we were still weak, at the right time Christ died for the ungodly. Why, one will hardly die for a righteous man—though perhaps for a good man one will dare even to die. But God shows his love for us in that while we were yet sinners Christ died for us. Since, therefore, we are now justified by his blood, much more shall we be saved by him from the wrath of God. For if while we were enemies we were reconciled to God by the death of his Son, much more, now that we are reconciled, shall we be saved by his life. Not only so, but we also rejoice in God through our Lord Jesus Christ, through whom we have now received our reconciliation.

Therefore as sin came into the world through one man and death through sin, and so death spread to all men because all men sinned—sin indeed was in the world before the law was given, but sin is not counted where there is no law. Yet death reigned from Adam to Moses, even over those whose sins were not like the transgression of Adam, who was a type of the one who was to come.

—Romans 5:6–14

3

Tear Off the Label

Leo Tolstoy once said, "All great revolutions in our life are made in thought. When a change takes place in man's thought, action follows the direction of the thought as a ship follows the direction of a rudder."

History bears him out. The twentieth century has been shaped, for good or ill, by four great revolutions, each of which began as an idea in the minds of four men living in the late nineteenth and early twentieth centuries: Charles Darwin, Sigmund Freud, Karl Marx, and Albert Einstein.

What began with an idea in someone's head, in time, rearranged the world. Even those who have never heard of Darwin or Freud or Marx or Einstein have had their lives affected by the revolutions their ideas ignited. When a change takes place in our minds, action follows the thought as a ship follows the direction of a rudder.

Because of the power of ideas, we can be optimistic about the future. We can build a better world if we make up our minds to do it. God has given us the resources and the tools. All we lack is the idea that we can do it. We still labor under old ideas about the world that tell us it can't happen. We point to the past and say there always have been wars, violence, hunger, and exploitation of others, so there always will be. But those evils persist not because we can't do anything about them, but because we think we can't. In a speech at the University of California reported by the *Saturday Review,* Archibald MacLeish said, "For man, as the whole of science as well as the whole of poetry, will demonstrate, is not what he thinks he knows, but what he thinks he *can* know, can become."

Franklin Jacobs is a young man, five feet eight inches tall, who weighs about one hundred and fifty pounds, and high jumps seven feet seven inches. He has a unique style of jumping, his own version of the "Fosbury Flop." He doesn't take off like an airplane and sail over the bar. He takes off like a helicopter, vertically, and pulls himself over the bar. It's crazy, but it works. A *Christian Science Monitor* reporter asked him how a man five feet eight inches tall could jump seven feet seven inches. He said, "Tallness is not measured in inches. It's determined by the state of your mind."

Karl Barth, who began his career with the *Epistle to the Romans* in which he emphasized Paul's realism about human sin, concluded his life work with a little book entitled *Christ and Adam,* in which he underscored human possibility. The book is a study of Romans 5. In it is an idea more explosive than any of those that transformed the twentieth century. Barth warned there was dynamite stored in this simple phrase: "Adam, who was a type of the one who was to come."

That means that Adam is not the true human being. He was just the first one. Christ is the true human being, the prototype for all human life. Christ, not Adam, is the model for your life and mine. Adam was just a type of the one who was to come, and a poor copy, as we are. Christ is the model. We are to be like Christ, not like Adam.

We were taught differently. We were taught that as descendants of Adam, we live our lives under some limitation or curse. "In Adam's fall we sinned all." We were told human nature is essentially sinful, human bodies essentially evil, and there was nothing we could do about it.

Even though we may not use the old language, we express the same idea in other ways. Every time I say, "I can't do anything about my life, that's just the way I am," I am saying that I believe in the "old Adam" theory of human nature. When I say, "The world will always be the way it is now," I am revealing that I believe that history exists under some curse.

The good news Paul gives to the Romans is that if we live like Adam, we do so by choice. By nature we are like Christ. Adam was simply a type of the one who was to come. The "one who was to come" was Jesus of Nazareth. He is the true human being, the model for you and me.

Now here is the dynamite. You can put aside "the old Adam," because there is no determinism, no curse, no taint, no guilt that you have to carry around with you the rest of your life. You can choose the way you live in this life. You choose whether you will live like Adam or put on Christ.

To live like Adam is to focus on the limitations of your life. Behavioral sciences have been a great help to us, but like all good things they often have a negative by-product. To be a science, psychology must objectively analyze human behavior, which involves ordering and classifying types. The destructive by-product of categorizing human beings is to fix labels on them, which come down upon them as a curse they must live with the rest of their lives.

In addition, society puts labels on us because of our race, or our size, or our vocation. They think they have us pegged. Because of the label they think they know who we are, but they don't.

We are also given labels such as "divorced," or "single," or "widowed," and the label determines what we think of ourselves and what is possible for us to achieve in this life.

When we live according to the labels other people or society place upon us, we are living as if we were condemned or cursed or predetermined into an existence that is not ours.

In Paul's time, people did the same thing. There were labels everywhere: publican and Pharisee, righteous and sinner, clean and unclean, Jew and Gentile, slave and free, male and female. The label was your fate. You had to be what the label said you were.

Into that world came this liberating news: You are not really any of these things. You are like Christ. All of us are like Christ. He is the true human being, the model, the prototype of which we are a type. So you can live like Adam, focusing on the limitations of human existence, or you can try to be like Christ and focus on the possibilities.

Now that is pretty heavy stuff, and it needs to be qualified. In the previous chapter we looked at Paul's realism about human sin. Becoming Christian, putting on Christ, does not mean that you are going to be free from sin. William H. Willimon, in his book *Worship as Pastoral Care,* recalled Luther's remark about baptism, "The old Adam is a mighty good swimmer." So don't think becoming Christian puts an end to the war that rages inside us.

In fact your life won't be that much different, not from what other people can see. They will look at you and think you are pretty much the same old person. What has changed is in your head—the image you have of yourself, the goals you have set for your life, the model you try to live by. That will be the difference, and that is where the difference counts.

In our house, given the traffic, one of the most effective means of communication is to leave a message on the refrigerator door. "Dad: Someone called. I didn't get his name. He wants you to call back." That kind of message. Also there are report cards up there, the good ones, and cartoons which serve as a gentle way to point out each other's idiosyncrasies. A couple of years ago a cartoon was placed on the refrigerator showing a middle-aged man wearing a T-shirt, walking down the street with a scowl on his face. On the shirt was printed, "Please don't ask me to have a nice day." I didn't know for whom that cartoon was intended, but the point is well taken. If you don't want to have a nice day, chances are you aren't going to have it. If you decide to have a nice day, chances are you are going to do the things to make it happen. Somebody said, "Optimists are wrong about as often as pessimists. The difference is they have more fun."

You can *will* to have a nice day because the world is still in the process of being created. There are always new possibilities. God isn't finished with the world yet, and God has given us power to help do it. That is why the book of Genesis says God gives us dominion over the creation (Gen. 1:26). It is also why Jesus, in his parables, uses the image of God as the master and us as the stewards who have power to make something good come out of life (Luke 12:41f; 16:1f).

The material given us may not be what we would have chosen ourselves. In the parable of the talents the master gives the servants different sums of money, called talents. The servants could have complained that they were not given what others have, but they didn't. The point of the parable is that life is not determined by what you have received, but by what you do with it (Matt. 25:14–30).

I can't always control whether I make mistakes. I can control whether I learn from the mistakes. I can't control other people's behavior, but I can control my attitude toward their behavior. I can't control whether something is going to shatter my dreams about life, but I can control whether I will stop dreaming. I can't always control whether I will suffer defeat in this life, but I can control whether I am going to be a defeatist.

That is what having dominion means. You can take the stuff that life gives you and make something good come out of it. Viktor Frankl talks about the last of the human freedoms as he experienced it in concentration camps during World War II. He said in *Man's Search for Meaning:* "Everything can be taken from a man but one thing: the last of the human freedoms—to choose one's attitude in any given circumstance."

Paul makes the same point. He doesn't say we can rid ourselves of the limitations on our life. We can't. But he talks about becoming more than conqueror over the limitations through Christ. Because Christ is the true human being, the prototype, we can stop talking about the limitations of being like Adam and start talking about the possibilities when we become like Christ.

III

Faithful Living

That is why it depends on faith, in order that the promise may rest on grace and be guaranteed to all his descendants—not only to the adherents of the law but also to those who share the faith of Abraham, for he is the father of us all, as it is written, "I have made you the father of many nations"—in the presence of the God in whom he believed, who gives life to the dead and calls into existence the things that do not exist. In hope he believed against hope, that he should become the father of many nations; as he had been told, "So shall your descendants be." He did not weaken in faith when he considered his own body, which was as good as dead because he was about a hundred years old, or when he considered the barrenness of Sarah's womb. No distrust made him waver concerning the promise of God, but he grew strong in his faith as he gave glory to God, fully convinced that God was able to do what he had promised.

—Romans 4:16–21

4

Living by Promises

Once there was a little man named Bilbo Baggins who went on a great adventure. He was a very common man, not the kind you would expect to do such a thing. He was, in fact, quite timid about adventuring outside the safety of his comfortable dwelling. His idea of a good evening was to sit in front of the fire, smoke his pipe, and read the newspaper. He was the kind of person who lived by a predictable schedule within a controlled environment.

But one day he left his secure life and ventured out into the world in search of a treasure. He faced many dangers and had many close shaves; but he finally came to the place of treasure, guarded by a dragon, which he slew.

When he returned home from his adventure, he was a different man. He was still Bilbo Baggins all right, but he wasn't the same. He had lost one life and found another. He was a new man. His adventure, his journey, had given him a new life.

You probably recognize Bilbo Baggins from *The Hobbit* by J. R. R. Tolkien. Tolkien was one of a group of writers at Cambridge University, including C. S. Lewis, who called themselves "The Inklings." They were dedicated to the resurrection of the fairy tale as serious English literature. As his contribution to that project, Tolkien wrote *The Hobbit* and related works and Lewis wrote *The Chronicles of Narnia*. Both men believed that fairy tales are not meant merely to entertain or frighten children, although many of them succeed in doing that. The real purpose of fairy tales is to teach children, and adults, how to live.

That is also the purpose of the Bible. The Bible does it with stories, not fairy tales, but stories of real human beings, men and women like you and me, common folk and unlikely candidates for adventure or greatness. Many, in fact, are overlooked because they do not have sufficient beauty or strength or leadership to cause anyone to pay attention to them.

But God pays attention to them and calls them to undertake a great mission in this life. When they respond faithfully, they receive a great blessing, the greatest treasure the world yields: the transformation of life. They become new persons.

There is one biblical hero who illustrates this lesson better than anyone else, and Paul holds that person up as our example. In the third chapter of Romans he says the Christian is the person who lives by faith alone. Now in the fourth chapter of Romans he illustrates what faith looks like, and says it looks like Abraham, who risked everything, left his comfortable home, and started on a great adventure in search of a promised land. Abraham faced many difficulties, dangers, and disappointments. Yet, Paul wrote, "No distrust made him waver concerning the promise of God, but he grew strong in his faith as he gave glory to God, fully convinced that God was able to do what he had promised" (Rom. 4:20–21). When Paul talks about faith, he points to Abraham, "the father of all who live by faith" (Rom. 4:16, author's paraphrase).

Four thousand years ago Abraham was living in a beautiful place called the Ur of the Chaldeans. It was part of the Fertile Crescent, that precious inhabitable land with good soil and abundant water. In the Ur of the Chaldeans the living was easy. Abraham had a good life in a good land. It was certainly much better than the life he was about to embark upon, a life of wandering as a nomad through the arid deserts of the Near East.

One day God came to Abraham and said, "I am going to give you and your descendants a great blessing, but first you have to let go of the life you're now living. It's going to be rough and there are going to be many dangers, toils, and snares, but in the end there will be a great blessing. And that's a promise'' (Gen. 12:1–3, author's paraphrase).

The story of Abraham in Genesis is held together by the tension of whether or not God will keep promises. Abraham encounters incredible difficulties and obstacles, not the least of which is the inability of his wife Sarah to have a son, an embarrassment to a man who has just been promised that his descendants will be as numerous as the stars in the heavens. But when Abraham is ninety-nine and Sarah is ninety, she gives birth to Isaac. It looks as if the promise has been kept and the treasure won. Then comes the terrible command to give up his only son, Isaac. Abraham continues to have faith in God and Isaac is spared. ''No distrust made him waver concerning the promise of God, but he grew strong in his faith as he gave glory to God, fully convinced that God was able to do what he had promised (Rom. 4:20–21).

In his book *The Courage to Be,* Paul Tillich defined faith as ''courage,'' a definition that conforms perfectly to this heroic model of faith in Abraham. We think of faith as a matter of the intellect that requires us to believe a lot of things. But faith is more a matter of doing. It's not a matter of the intellect so much as a matter of the will. Faith is the courage to keep on going, trusting God's promise that life will always be good no matter what happens. Faith is the courage to keep on going when the promise of your life is threatened.

Did you ever notice that the heroes in fairy tales are very often children? I suppose it is that way so that children can identify with them. But it also is that way so that adults can see how they are supposed to be. Jesus held up the same model when he said that unless you become like children you cannot inherit the kingdom of God. Unless you approach life with the faith of children, you will not discover the treasure that is hidden in this world for you.

In the book *Pilgrim at Tinker Creek,* Annie Dillard calls our attention to an infant who has just learned how to hold his head upright. He sits there and gazes starkly in awe and wonder at the world. He hasn't the faintest idea of where he is, but he aims to find out. He's going to be an explorer. He looks at everything. He picks things up and throws them down to see what happens. She says we are born to be explorers and pilgrims, adventurers, risk-takers. It is as if when we are born we are given a secret that a treasure is hidden in this world somewhere, and our purpose for being here is to find it. Or, as if we receive a promise as we begin our pilgrimage that there will be a great blessing, so we start out as children with enthusiasm, excitement, and exhilaration. We cannot wait to begin the pilgrimage, to receive the blessing.

But then look what happens. After a short time we learn how to fake it. We become squatters who think we own the place. We don't explore the world anymore. We defend our little space. We don't welcome the new anymore. We are suspicious of anything that is strange to us. And we stop asking questions. We believe that preposterous notion that our tiny brain and our puny experience can provide us with all the answers we need. But we didn't start out that way. We started out exploring and adventuring and risking, as if there were a treasure in this life and our reason for being here is to look about us, to examine everything, until we find it. But after a while we get tired of surmounting obstacles, feeling pain, facing dangers, and suffering humiliation. So we play it safe and withdraw, stay put, and stop moving.

My first attempt at skiing was an adventure. While my wife Jean and I were living in Boston, we went to New Hampshire for a weekend of skiing with some friends. I have a lot of Bilbo in me, and because this was something I had never done before, I feared something terrible would happen. My fear found what it was looking for.

When we arrived at the resort, as a beginner I was told to go over to the "bunny hill." It was about the size of a pitcher's mound, with children swarming all over it. After I mastered the "bunny hill," I was graduated to a larger slope, which was ascended by means of a tow rope.

That looked simple enough, so I grabbed the rope and started up the hill. Nearing the top I noticed that when I reached the summit I would have to let go. I didn't know what I was supposed to do after I let go, but when you reach the top you have no choice, so I let go. And I wish that I could claim that I skied away like Jean-Claude Killy, but I skied like me. Actually, I didn't ski at all. The moment I let go I fell, the skis revolving around my head. I looked like a disabled helicopter. Then the final embarrassment. All those kids on the tow rope, one by one, tumbled over me. I've never been skiing again.

It doesn't take many experiences like that—venturing forth into the strange and the new, starting out on an adventure and failing miserably at it, being embarrassed or getting hurt—to convince you that you're better off to play it safe. You come away vowing to cling to the familiar. You are convinced that from here on you will say no to the changes in life.

Faith is courage. And the opposite of faith is fear. We think that doubt is the opposite of faith but it's not. Most doubt is healthy and will lead to new life. Doubt will get a squatter searching again. Doubt is not the opposite of faith. Fear is the opposite of faith. Fear is paralyzing and it will end your life.

I have a cartoon showing two birds sitting on a branch. One bird is wearing a parachute. The other bird says, "Sheldon, the trouble with you is you lack self-confidence." It's kind of silly for a bird to wear a parachute, but it's not only silly, it's pathetic for men and women created to be pilgrims in this world in search of a treasure, to spend their lives as squatters defending their territory.

"Consider the birds of the air," Jesus said. They wear no parachutes. They trust that the air is going to hold them up. So why do we fear that if we leave our little nests we are going to be destroyed?

Have you ever noticed how cautious the wisdom of the world is? That's why the Bible contrasts the wisdom of the world with the foolishness of faith. Paul makes a great deal of that. He writes, "We are fools for Christ's sake" (1 Cor. 4:10). The wisdom of the world says play it safe. Look after yourself. Defend your territory. Don't budge. Whatever you do, don't move. The foolishness of faith says give and you shall receive. Lose your life in order to find it. Don't hold onto what you think are certainties, but let go and live by promises.

Paul saw the danger that the church would preach the wisdom

of the world rather than the foolishness of Christ. The church is always tempted to nurse our fears rather than embolden our courage. When Christianity appears negative, narrow, provincial, dogmatic, mean, and self-centered, it is playing to the fears of people rather than trying to get them to live with courage. Consider this little verse:

> Our fathers have been churchmen
> Two thousand years or so
> And to every new proposal
> They have always answered no.

Why is it that we think "no" is more appropriately religious than "yes"? If you ask a religious person his opinion of some new idea, almost nine out of ten times that person will say no to it, simply because it's new. He thinks he's being faithful, but he's just being fearful. Why is it that when the new comes along people always expect the church to be against it? Because of fear. When our life changes—we lose our job, the one we depend upon betrays us, we enter into a period of sorrow, or we start out on an adventure and meet the first goblin in the netherwood—why do we retreat and hide? Because we are afraid.

And we turn to the church to comfort us. But the purpose of Christian faith is to encourage us. We want to say no to what has happened to us, but the vocabulary of faith is yes, as in Dag Hammarskjöld's beautiful prayer in *Markings,* so light, incidentally, that pilgrims can carry it on their journey:

> "—Night is drawing nigh—"
> For all that has been—Thanks!
> To all that shall be—Yes!

God gives heroes of the Bible very little comfort. Sideshow religion sells comfort. Comfort is the theme of so many of the hymns that are sung in the church. The "comfortable words" are the ones we select from the lectionary. That's all right. They are there and they ought to be read. But you also ought to read the stories of the heroes in the Bible, the pilgrims of faith. Surprisingly, God treats them roughly. To the complaining Job, God says, "Stand up on your feet like a man, I have something to show you." To Elijah who is hiding from Jezebel in a cave, God says, "Get out of here. I have something better for you to do with your life." To Moses, hiding on his father-in-law's farm in Midian, not wanting to go back to the dangers of Egypt, complaining that he can't be a leader, God says, "I don't care if you don't think you're a leader, I'll tell you what to do." And then to Paul, plagued by some thorn in his flesh for which he was given no answer, just the words, "Keep on going, and I'll give you strength. My grace is sufficient for you."

These are heroes of faith the Bible holds up as our examples, and they are heroes because they have the courage to keep on going when it appears that the promise of their life is threatened. They are the examples of what faith looks like. As is our Lord who, living the life of a pilgrim, left his home in Nazareth, went to the River Jordan to be baptized, then went out to the desert for forty days and nights, wandered the roads of Palestine with no place to lay his head, set his face steadfastly for Jerusalem, and there walked the *Via Dolorosa*. He traveled through many dangers and disappointments until he came finally on Friday to that dragon called death . . . which he slew.

And now Jesus says to use, "Follow me." Paul asks, do you want to know what it looks like to follow him? It looks like Abraham, the father of all who have faith. "No distrust made him waver concerning the promise of God, but he grew strong in his faith as he gave glory to God, fully convinced that God was able to do what he had promised" (Rom. 4:20,21).

Therefore, since we are justified by faith, we have peace with God through our Lord Jesus Christ. Through him we have obtained access to this grace in which we stand, and we rejoice in our hope of sharing the glory of God. More than that, we rejoice in our sufferings, knowing that suffering produces endurance, and endurance produces character, and character produces hope, and hope does not disappoint us, because God's love has been poured into our hearts through the Holy Spirit which has been given to us.

—Romans 5:1–5

5

A Severe Mercy

Millions of Christians inside Russia today are free to practice their faith within the guidelines set by the government. But they pay a price for it. Many jobs are not available to them; they are passed over for promotions and denied privileges granted to others.

Among the Russian Christians about a million evangelicals refuse even to abide by the guidelines, particularly that law which prohibits "proselytizing," but what they, as Christians, call evangelism. These Christians pay a greater price. Thousands are in prison and still more are in hiding.

Recently a tape cassette was smuggled out of Russia. The voice on the tape belonged to a man named Gennady Kryuchkov, the leader of the Reformed Baptists, one of the outlawed branches of Christianity in Russia. He is among those evangelicals who have gone underground. The voice on the tape says, as quoted in the *Christian Science Monitor,* "For ten years I have been hiding so that often I never see the sun. But there is great joy. We are fortunate to be Christians in the Soviet Union today."

Max Cleland is a United Methodist layman from Georgia. In 1968 in Vietnam he took the full force of a grenade that left him a triple amputee. After eighteen months rehabilitation, he returned home, entered politics, and was elected to the state senate. In

1977, Jimmy Carter appointed him director of the Veteran's Administration.

Max Cleland is a remarkable man, full of energy and optimism. He has a strong desire to serve. He will tell you that his faith in God not only enabled him to survive those difficult years of hospitalization and rehabilitation, but to receive a new purpose and meaning for his life. He entered the hospital in despair; he left with faith. The inscription on Robert Kennedy's grave, he said, summarized what he learned in the hospital:

> In our sleep, pain that cannot forget
> falls drop by drop
> Upon the heart, and in our despair
> against our will comes
> Wisdom through the awful Grace of God.

Sheldon and Jean Vanauken had a marriage of delicate and unusual beauty. He wrote that being married to Jean was like living in a perpetual springtime. They were committed Christians whose belief in God deepened and enriched the communion they had as husband and wife. They were also among the numerous people who have come under the influence of C. S. Lewis, whom they met when Sheldon was studying at Cambridge University where Lewis taught medieval literature.

Not long after they returned to America, Jean was stricken with a fatal disease. When she died, Sheldon turned to Lewis for counsel through the period of sorrow. They corresponded extensively on the meaning of suffering and the will of God. In one of his letters, Lewis wrote, "You have been treated with a severe mercy."

Part of what Lewis is saying by describing Vanauken's sorrow as a severe mercy is that life is hard, and if you think it is going to be a perpetual springtime, you are kidding yourself. After the youthful, playful innocence of spring, inevitably comes the withering heat of summer, the senescence of autumn, and the death of winter. Life is severe, and if you are going to rest your happiness on life being gentle to you, the chances are you are going to end up in despair.

On the other hand, there are the testimonies of men and women such as Kryuchkov in his hiding place and Cleland in his wheelchair to a strange mercy in their struggle. Their lives were harsh. We wouldn't trade places with any of them, yet they experienced a quality of grace in their suffering most of us have never known. The severity of their suffering was graced with a strange mercy.

Their testimony is similar to Paul's affirmation: "We rejoice in our sufferings, knowing that suffering produces endurance, and endurance produces character, and character produces hope, and hope does not disappoint us" (Rom. 5:3–5). Suffering, he says, is not for nothing. It can be a severe mercy, the painful journey to a new life.

Look at his tightly spun argument: We rejoice in our suffering knowing that suffering produces endurance. Enduring suffering is not one of our favorite things to do. Most of us would probably edit Paul to read, "Suffering produces pain, and pain isn't good for anything."

As I was growing up adults used to tell me, "Suffering is good for you, so get out there and mow the lawn, or work the algebra problems. Stop complaining about the hurt, be a man." The dentist was one of those who believed suffering was good for you. He had a drill that worked at about six revolutions per minute. When he got me in his chair, he would ask, "You don't want any novocaine, do you?" And, of course, wanting to be a man, I would say no, endure the suffering, and wait for some spiritual blessing. It never came.

In those days there were still some who assumed that by virtue of being human, you would have to endure pain in small or large amounts in this life. But technology has changed all that. In succession came labor-saving devices—luxury cars, painkillers, credit cards, electric blankets, and air conditioning—each one at first considered a luxury, then a necessity, and eventually an inalienable right. Our value system in one generation has undergone a radical transformation—from the expectation of suffering to the right of comfort. The religious crisis occurs when we expect Christianity to support that value system.

Someone sent me a book about a young, athletic, beautiful girl who was critically injured in an automobile accident and not expected to live. The book was about her miraculous recovery brought about by her parents' faith and prayers. I rejoice with that family. But as I read the book, I must admit I also winced at the suggestion that the girl's healing was the effect of her parents' faith. I believe that God healed that girl, because I believe that all healing is a gift from God. But not everybody is healed. Many aren't. And we are all healed to suffer another sickness, and, in time, a sickness from which we won't be healed.

All healing is a gift from God, but God has greater gifts than healing to give, and one of them is endurance, the courage to go on, as Paul did, with a thorn in your flesh, never to have it removed, not ever, and to keep on rejoicing. If you want to see a gift of God, that's it. As great a miracle as you will ever see are those who don't postpone rejoicing until the suffering passes, but who rejoice in their suffering.

Faith is not there to exempt you from suffering. It is there to encourage you in your suffering. They used to say suffering is good for you. Well, I don't believe it. Suffering is not good for you. Suffering can be injurious to your health. Faith is what is good for you. To mix faith with suffering produces endurance.

Paul says, "Endurance produces character." *Character* is a Greek word. In Greek it is a verb meaning "to engrave," to take a hammer and a chisel and chip away a rock. To *character* means to sculpt a shapeless stone into a beautiful work of art. *Character* means to have reached that point in life when enduring suffering faithfully has engraved a strange beauty upon your life.

Endurance does not always produce character. Enduring suffering may produce cynicism. I have seen people come back from war, not as better persons but with corrupted spirits. I have seen written on the faces of people, not character but suffering, not beauty but a terrible bitterness. So endurance does not always produce character. Only faithful endurance produces character.

Henry Mitchell, in *The Recovery of Preaching,* a helpful book about black preaching in America, pointed out that black religion did more praising than the religion of the white slave master. White religion in America in those days was a stern religion of law, sin, and judgment. Black religion, by contrast, was jubilant, joyful, and optimistic. Mitchell makes an interesting point. "I was convinced that African captives didn't go crazy because, despite the vast majority of cruel suffering in their lives, they focused consciousness on their few blessings." In other words, they used their religion to develop their character rather than to curse their suffering. Mitchell says they turned to passages written from prison by another captive named Paul: "Finally, brethren, whatever is true, whatever is honorable, whatever is just, whatever is pure, whatever is lovely, whatever is gracious, if there is any excellence, if there is anything worthy of praise, think about these things" (Phil. 4:8). The secret of black survival in slavery was that they held to the highest they knew while enduring the worst that could happen to them. Because they endured their suffering faithfully, their endurance produced character. Their suffering carved a strange kind of beauty in their lives, visible even today in the heritage they passed on to all Americans.

And finally, character produces hope. People who have tested their faith in adversity don't panic every time something goes wrong because they have learned they can rely on God's promise. They don't despair that some new crisis always seems to be lurking in the wings. They wait patiently for the promise of God to be fulfilled in their lives.

Samuel H. Miller could turn an aphorism as cleverly as C. S. Lewis. In *Religion in a Technical Age,* he wrote, "There is something inimical to the spirit in speed." Speed and religion don't mix. God isn't in a hurry. We are the ones who are in a hurry. God always moves at his own pace.

Perhaps that is why Americans today are having so much difficulty with traditional religion and why we chase after the sideshows. Technology has led us to expect to get what we want when we want it. We will give something a try, but if it doesn't work quickly or easily, we will try something else.

Many people go to church in time of trouble and never go back.

Perhaps they believe that if they go to church something wonderful will happen in their lives: the sorrow will pass, the prayer will be answered, the confusion will be removed. But they leave untouched and unmoved. They should stay awhile and be patient. But we are so attuned to instant gratification that we can't sit still.

In his play *St. Joan,* George Bernard Shaw pictures Joan of Arc talking with the Dauphin. He complains to her that he doesn't hear the voice she hears. She says, "They come to you, too, but you don't listen. You have not sat in the field in the evening and considered their message. When the Angelus rings you cross yourself and run off." We are like that. We give it a try and then we give it up.

Speed is inimical to religion. Patience is the essence of religion. Christians can be patient because they know God keeps promises. They don't panic when things go wrong. They wait on the Lord. Isaiah described the patience of the faithful:

> But they who wait for the Lord shall renew their strength,
>> they shall mount up with wings like eagles,
> they shall run and not be weary,
>> they shall walk and not faint.
>
> —Isaiah 40:31

We might paraphrase it this way: They shall read the latest headlines and not despair. They shall hear about the latest catastrophe and know that the world is not coming to an end. They shall hear about the latest scandal in government and know that we will get through this, too. They shall suffer a personal disappointment and know there will be another chance.

That is what hope looks like. Hope is not wishful thinking, hope is patience, waiting on the Lord, knowing that God keeps promises.

A *Christian Science Monitor* interviewer reminding Mortimer Adler, the philosopher and writer, that he had gone through a series of depressions in his life, asked him, "What sustained you through them?" Adler answered, "There have been two or three occasions when I was desperately unhappy. I stopped working or thinking. I couldn't see any light ahead and did not know whence the light would come. But the light did come and the clouds cleared. I did not do it by any devices of my own. Suddenly a door opened. If you live long enough, you learn to be patient.''

You need only to live long enough to know that you live by grace. The future doesn't depend on us or on our devices. The future depends on God, and God keeps the promise to be with us. So if we are patient, and attentive, if we wait on the Lord, a door will open.

For that reason we rejoice in our sufferings, for suffering produces endurance, endurance produces character, and character produces hope, and hope never disappoints.

This is the reason why I have so often been hindered from coming to you. But now, since I no longer have any room for work in these regions, and since I have longed for many years to come to you, I hope to see you in passing as I go to Spain, and to be sped on my journey there by you, once I have enjoyed your company for a little. At present, however, I am going to Jerusalem with aid for the saints. For Macedonia and Achaia have been pleased to make some contributions for the poor among the saints at Jerusalem; they were pleased to do it, and indeed they are in debt to them, for if the Gentiles have come to share in their spiritual blessings, they ought also to be of service to them in material blessings. When therefore I have completed this, and have delivered to them what has been raised, I shall go on by way of you to Spain; and I know that when I come to you I shall come in the fulness of the blessing of Christ.

—Romans 15:22–29

6

Dreams and Detours

Moses had a dream that someday he would live in the Promised Land. The one thing that kept him going through forty years of deprivation in the desert was the dream. And now he is an old man, standing on Mt. Nebo, looking across the River Jordan to the city of Jericho (Deut. 34:1–8).

Jericho was called the "city of palms." You can imagine what that sight meant for a man who had been on the desert all those years. Beyond Jericho he could see the whole horizon of the land of Canaan, the land that had been promised to his forefathers, Abraham, Isaac, and Jacob. He knew at last he had come to the fulfillment of his dreams.

But God said to Moses, "I will let you see it with your eyes, but you shall not go over there." Moses was too old, time had run out for him. He had spent his whole life pursuing the dream, and he died just short of it, in Moab, not on Canaan's side.

That poignant scene at the end of the life of Moses is reminiscent of Paul's personal word to the Romans: "Since I have longed for many years to come to you, I hope to see you in passing as I go to Spain" (Rom. 15:23–24). To go to Spain was the goal of Paul's life. He had dreamed of doing that for years, but something was always coming up. "I hope to see you in passing as I go to Spain. . . . At present, however, I am going to Jerusalem" (Rom. 15:24–25).

He did, and there he was arrested and taken to Rome to be

tried. There in Rome he stood like Moses on Mt. Nebo, so close to Spain he could almost see it, but the dream would not come true. He spent two years under arrest in Rome, and then, tradition says, during the Neronian persecutions he was beheaded.

Once again, Paul's life provides the example of faithful living. First, never stop dreaming. I suppose that is the secret of growing old. A great dream kept Moses going for a hundred and twenty years.

Toscanini was one of the great conductors of this century. When he was eighty-eight years old, he was invited to conduct the BBC orchestra in the great Albert Hall in London. After a spectacular performance, the board of trustees of the BBC quickly met and decided that they would invite Toscanini to be the orchestra's permanent conductor. They offered him a contract for two years. Toscanini looked at it and said, "I'm disappointed. I was hoping the contract would be for ten years."

Never stop dreaming. Never stop moving toward the promised life. Those who orient their lives to the future never stop living in the present.

Richard Strout, Washington correspondent for the *Christian Science Monitor,* recently wrote about what it was like to ride with Harry Truman's train through the west in the 1948 presidential election. He said it was one of the most haphazard, hectic, and disorganized affairs in modern United States history. In one town Truman dedicated an airport to the wrong person. He came to San Diego that summer and mixed his metaphors in his usual inimitable style saying, "Your population is going to come to the saturation point if you don't get some water down here." Truman talked with mixed metaphors and non sequiturs and malapropisms, and nobody came to hear him. He would speak to two thousand in an auditorium with ten thousand seats. Strout quoted *Life* magazine's description of Truman in those dog days of the summer of '48: "The most impressive thing last week about President Truman's trip to the west was his incredible ability to pretend that nothing at all was going wrong."

I imagine that is what the Hebrews thought about old Moses,

say twenty years into the Exodus, cursing him for what he was doing to them, ruing the day they ever let Moses liberate them. The fleshpots of Egypt looked pretty good to those who were starving and withering out there on the desert. But Moses just kept going, saying, "We're going to make it." He had this incredible ability to pretend that nothing at all was going wrong. The dream kept him going.

Paul was the same way. They warned him that if he went to Jerusalem he would probably never leave there. He had too many enemies lying in wait for him. But he went anyway, promising himself that when he finished his business in Jerusalem he would finally go to Spain. He must have known what was going on. He wasn't naïve. But he kept going on . . . as if nothing was going to go wrong.

I have seen people like that—people who don't care what the polls say, but who believe what they think is right; people who don't care what the doctor says, but who just keep on living; people who don't care what other people say, but who try to become the persons they think God wants them to be. They just keep on going, pretending that nothing at all is going wrong, holding to the dream, following Jesus' advice, "Seek ye first the kingdom of God, and his righteousness; and all these things shall be added unto you" (Matt. 6:33, KJV).

Secondly, expect detours. That advice to hold to the dream is not exclusively Christian, you know. You can read that in any self-help psychology book. Most of the advice will tell you to keep on dreaming in spite of everything else. In other words, think only of yourself.

Paul presents us with a different image. He says, "I have longed for many years to come to you. I hope to see you on my way to Spain, but first I have to go to Jerusalem to deliver the offering to the saints."

Paul had a responsibility to fulfill in Jerusalem. The church was threatening to split in two, the Jewish Christians on one side and the Gentile Christians on the other. The Jewish Christians believed you had to become a Jew in order to become Christian.

They taught that Christians were to abide by Jewish laws. The Gentile Christians believed that Christ freed them from obedience to those laws. The church was splitting apart over that issue. Although Paul sided with the Gentile Christians, he tried to keep the church united.

The center of Jewish Christianity was the mother church in Jerusalem. As a gesture of reconciliation and unity, Paul took up an offering among the Gentile churches for the poor people in the church at Jerusalem. He felt it was his personal duty to deliver the offering to them. Ignoring the warnings of his friends of the danger, he went to Jerusalem and postponed his dream of going to Spain.

His example shows us that if we keep our eyes on the kingdom of God, if we seek that first, then the shortest distance to the kingdom may not be a straight line. It may involve detours.

It was put plainly in a quote from Henri Nouwen's writing in one of his books, *Reaching Out*. While he was visiting the University of Notre Dame, a professor said to Nouwen, "You know, . . . my whole life I have been complaining that my work was constantly interrupted, until I learned that my interruptions were my work."

That is exactly what Paul is telling us. It is a lesson I have had to learn in my own life. I am one of those compulsive people who makes lists of all the things I am supposed to do. If I don't write it down I'll forget it, and then, of course, I forget to look at the list. Most of the time the list comprises the things I feel I must do in order to get to the things I want to do. The greatest joy for somebody like me is to come to the last item on that list, crumple up the paper, and throw it away. It seldom happens. There are always more things to do.

Something is always taking us away from our dreams. We have to go to Jerusalem. Some need makes a claim upon the savings we had put aside for the trip. Our responsibility to parents, or children, means we can't do what we would like to do.

If you choose to live the life of faith, the life that Paul outlines for us and of which he is the model, then you had better expect to take detours from time to time. Don't stop dreaming about the future. Faith instructs us to do that. But at the same time, don't neglect the responsibilities that come to us in the present.

The other day I was watching one of those TV magazine shows on which an entertainer was being interviewed. I don't remember who he was, but I will never forget what he said. He was talking about the priorities in his life and how important success was for him. As an illustration, he told of a phone call he had received recently from his mother informing him that his father had died, and asking him to come home for the funeral. And this man, with all his priorities intact, told his mother, no. It would take away from his rehearsing.

Something has gone out of our lives when the dreams of the future blind us to the responsibilities in the present. Jesus taught us something about that in the parable of the good Samaritan. He said that the man or woman of faith is the person who is willing to be detoured in order to face responsibilities, especially those we owe one another. He taught us that the interruptions may be our proper work.

That doesn't lessen the importance of dreaming. Faith encourages us to dream about a better life in the future. But faith also awakens us to the importance of meeting the responsibilities in the present.

Holding that balance—that tension between the future and the present, between dreaming and responsibility—is the secret of a successful life. The person who can do that lives well. That is what faith enables you to do. Faith encourages you to keep on dreaming, and faith compels you to remember the responsibilities you have for others. Paraphrasing Paul,

> I long to come to you on my way to Spain. But first I must go to Jerusalem to deliver the offering to the saints.

IV

Life in the Spirit

But you are not in the flesh, you are in the Spirit, if in fact the Spirit of God dwells in you. Any one who does not have the Spirit of Christ does not belong to him. But if Christ is in you, although your bodies are dead because of sin, your spirits are alive because of righteousness. If the Spirit of him who raised Jesus from the dead dwells in you, he who raised Christ Jesus from the dead will give life to your mortal bodies also through his Spirit which dwells in you.

So then, brethren, we are debtors, not to the flesh, to live according to the flesh—for if you live according to the flesh you will die, but if by the Spirit you put to death the deeds of the body you will live. For all who are led by the Spirit of God are sons of God. For you did not receive the spirit of slavery to fall back into fear, but you have received the spirit of sonship. When we cry, "Abba! Father!" it is the Spirit himself bearing witness with our spirit that we are children of God, and if children, then heirs, heirs of God and fellow heirs with Christ, provided we suffer with him in order that we may also be glorified with him.

—Romans 8:9–17

7

We Are Not Alone

The producers of the film *Close Encounters of the Third Kind* knew what they were doing. The advertisements for the movie showed a picture of the planet earth set over against the void of space. Written across the ad were the words, ''We Are Not Alone.'' That is the most profoundly religious announcement that could be made to this generation.

The way the gospel is preached has changed many times. The gospel is the same, but the language used, the way it is spoken to each generation, is determined by the needs of that generation.

In an earlier age people asked the question, ''What is my status before a stern and righteous God?'' To those people the answer was, ''You are righteous in the presence of God through grace.'' Some still ask that question, and for them the old language retains its power to save.

But increasingly the religious problem is not phrased, Does God forgive me? but, Does God know of my existence? In an earlier age people felt guilt and sought forgiveness. The twentieth-century experience is more likely to be estrangement and loneliness, and the need is for relationship.

Human beings used to sit pretty in this universe. They believed that the planet earth was fixed immovably in the center of the universe. The sun, they believed, traveled around the earth. The clouds—just a little above us—formed a canopy, soft and billowy, so angels could lie down and be comfortable as they watched over us. And God's throne was nestled up there in the clouds, within shouting distance.

Today many people see the world differently. They no longer think that the planet earth is at the center of the universe, but is merely one insignificant pebble on the infinite beach. Before, it was believed that the whole universe was visible to the eye. Now the whole universe is incomprehensible to the mind.

Awareness of the insignificance of the world in an infinite universe leads people to ask how God could possibly know of their existence, much less know me personally. These people are not likely to ask, "Are my sins forgiven?" They don't feel close enough to God to feel guilt. The question they ask is, "Am I important? Does my life count? Does God really know that I exist?"

The age in which we live began in the latter part of the last century when the full impact of modern science hit home. As usual it was the artists, those with the most sensitive antennae, who gave advanced warning of what was happening. One of the first to do so was Matthew Arnold, who stood on the cliffs of Dover, watched the tide ebb, and wrote his famous poem, "Dover Beach,"

> The Sea of Faith
> Was once, too, at the full, and round earth's shore
> Lay like the folds of a bright gridle furl'd.
> But now I only hear
> Its melancholy, long, withdrawing roar,
> Retreating, to the breath
> Of the night-wind, down the vast edges drear
> And naked shingles of the world.

In the closing lines of that poem he gave this haunting description of a world that lives without faith in God.

> Ah, love, let us be true
> To one another! for the world, which seems
> To lie before us like a land of dreams,

WE ARE NOT ALONE

So various, so beautiful, so new,
Hath really neither joy, nor love, nor light,
Nor certitude, nor peace, nor help for pain;
And we are here as on a darkling plain
Swept with confused alarms of struggle and flight,
Where ignorant armies clash by night.

In previous ages people wondered how they stood in relation to a righteous God. Now they fear that they stand alone, on a darkling plain, with no certitude, no peace, and no help for pain.

At the threshold of this century, in 1899, a Norwegian painter, Edvard Munch, exhibited a painting he called "The Cry," which some critics label "the twentieth-century painting." A man is on a bridge, his face contorted with fear, his head held in his hands, his mouth open in a cry. In the background is a silhouette of a man and woman walking away from him, completely oblivious to the man with the cry. Is it a silent scream? Or is it that they can't hear him? The sky and sea and the land that frame the scene seem to be collapsing in upon the man who cries without being heard.

In a *Christian Science Monitor* article, Theodore Wolff said of this painting, "What differentiates our age from those of the past is that in this one we have been rudely awakened in the darkest hour of the night, and are sitting up with a wildly beating heart listening intently for something both within ourselves and without."

Those movie producers knew what they were doing. In another age the gospel may have been, "You are forgiven," but in our age, increasingly, the Good News is heard as, "We are not alone." Your cries are heard. There is still joy and certitude. There is still peace and help for pain.

Theologians talk about the amazing providence that Jesus came into our world when and where and in the way he did. Palestine was at the crossroads of two great civilizations of the ancient world, the Jewish and the Greek. The first Christian preaching was addressed to both the Jews with their stern morality, and to the Greeks with their fatalism and despair.

Paul speaks to both cultures. It is as if the fifth chapter, with its

79

language of justification through faith in God's grace, is for the Jews, and the eighth chapter, with its message of the Spirit, is for the Greeks. The fifth chapter uses the language of jurisprudence, the eighth chapter uses the language of family.

> For all who are led by the Spirit of God are sons of God. For you did not receive the spirit of slavery to fall back into fear, but you have received the spirit of sonship. When we cry, ''Abba! Father!'' it is the Spirit himself bearing witness with our spirit that we are children of God, and if children, then heirs, heirs of God and fellow heirs with Christ, provided we suffer with him in order that we may also be glorified with him.
>
> —Romans 8:14–17

It is no accident that so-called ''spirit religion'' or ''Pentecostalism'' is rapidly growing today. To have the Spirit of God touch your spirit is to know that you are not alone, that you have a certitude that nobody can take away, peace that passes understanding, and a balm for the pain in your life. It wasn't too long ago that some were prophesying the end of religion and the triumph of the secular. But religion has not declined. It has increased, particularly that religion that promises that the Spirit will touch our spirit. Pentecostalism, which had a bad reputation until recently, now has gained respectability, because so many people seek overwhelming and ecstatic experiences of the Spirit.

There are many who believe the Spirit of God has not touched their spirit. They have not had, and do not seek, a Pentecostal-type experience. This passage is addressed to them. It suggests that the Spirit of God touches our spirits with the experience of assurance, similar to what Wesley reported happened to him at Aldersgate. In those moments when we are up against the extremity of life or are confronted with our significance or become aware of our impotence to accomplish what we want in this life, then, if we are quiet and attentive, the Spirit brushes our spirit with the graceful assurance, ''You are a child of God.''

It may happen the way it came to G. Studdert Kennedy, who stood on an English shore, as Matthew Arnold had stood before him. But Kennedy was acutely sensitive to God's mysterious presence. He was alone. The dark vault of heaven with a million stars above, the only sound the sound of waves beating against the cliffs. He was totally alone, and yet acutely conscious of Another, a "vast mysterious presence other than himself moving out there in the dark."

He felt that night as he felt on another night, years later when he was fighting in France in World War I, lying between the trenches in no-man's land, as he saw a figure moving in the darkness, coming toward him, not knowing if it was friend or enemy. If he whispered, "Who goes there?" would the answer be a bullet, a friendly voice, or silence? So that night by the sea he thought, "Suppose I call out 'Who goes there?' Would there be any answer, or would there just be silence and the sound of the waves and the wind?" He decided to cry out, as related in Wallace Hamilton's *Who Goes There?*

> I got my answer. I have sometimes doubted it, have never wholly understood it, but it remains. If I lost it I think I would lose my soul. I have been trying to say it ever since, one word—God. I stood that night in the presence of God.

You and I have had experiences that we can neither understand nor explain away. Few have been overwhelming. Most of them have been quiet, reassuring experiences, coming when we were aware of our insignificance against the vast impersonality of life.

For some it will come as hope that there will be a chance for a new life. If I will just continue searching, eventually the doors that have been closed to me will open. For others it will come as strength to keep struggling to be free of a demonic habit that is ruining their lives. For others it will come as a challenge to accomplish something in their life they never thought they would be able to do. For still others it will be the courage to take the first step toward reconciliation with somebody else. And most often I have seen it as the courage to face the end of life with the knowledge that because we have the assurance that we are children of God, death is but a homecoming.

When the Spirit leads our spirit, it will probably be like that. It will not be a dramatic, jolting experience, but a quiet assurance when you are alone, that you really are not alone at all. Or when you are confronted with the vast impersonality of things, you will know that you are important. And when it appears you have come to the end of your strength, and the world is coldly indifferent to your wants and deaf to your cries, you will discover power that you did not know you had.

Lillian Smith was one of the great writers of this century. For fourteen years she fought cancer with a series of operations and cobalt and hormone treatments. She kept on going. She had one other blow during those years, one that would discourage anybody else. Her house burned down and she lost a completed manuscript for a book, parts of other manuscripts, and a whole lifetime of her correspondence. Her editor, George P. Brockway, in his book *You Do It Because You Love Somebody,* pointed out that she kept going strong despite this keen disappointment. He recalled that she published four new books, new editions of two other books, and wrote enough speeches and articles to make a stack "three thousand to four thousand pages high." She wrote:

> One wants to yowl sometimes, at this never ending struggle. It has to be; God, I wish I were as courageous as my friends think I am.

Another time she wrote:

> The experience of facing my awesome anxiety, then the things you go through again and again . . . then death, learning not to fear it really, anymore, learning that pain can actually be forgotten especially when one is writing or concerned about others; learning that there is a strange energy inside one that pulls, pulls, pulls.

Call it what you will, but Paul would say that strange energy that pulls inside of you is the Spirit of God touching your spirit, to tell you that you are a child of God.

Likewise the Spirit helps us in our weakness; for we do not know how to pray as we ought, but the Spirit himself intercedes for us with sighs too deep for words. And he who searches the hearts of men knows what is the mind of the Spirit, because the Spirit intercedes for the saints according to the will of God.

We know that in everything God works for good with those who love him, who are called according to his purpose. For those whom he foreknew he also predestined to be conformed to the image of his Son, in order that he might be the first-born among many brethren. And those whom he predestined he also called; and those whom he called he also justified; and those whom he justified he also glorified.

—Romans 8:26–30

8

The Man with a Tongue of Wood

A man down in Texas is a professional pray-er. For a fee he will come to your convention and dazzle you with his invocation. His pious eloquence has made him famous, earned him a nice living, pleased his audiences, and brought him close to blasphemy.

He flirts with blasphemy because he makes prayer a performance, the very thing Jesus condemned when he saw Pharisees praying in public so they could be seen by men. Jesus' instruction to us was, "When you pray, go into your room and shut the door" (Matt. 6:6a).

Many years ago an article appeared in a Boston newspaper which included this "review": "Rev. Parker prayed the finest prayer ever delivered to a Boston audience." Prayer is supposed to be delivered to God, not an audience—even if they be Bostonians. To use prayer as a performance is to skirt blasphemy.

Professional prayer is dangerous for another reason. It reinforces the misconception that prayer is easy and that if we stumble and stammer we aren't really praying. Have you ever had that experience? Have you ever said, "I don't know what to say when I pray?" Have you ever been asked to pray in public and found that the words just didn't come? Well listen to Paul's analysis of our condition.

Likewise the Spirit helps us in our weakness; for we do not know how to pray as we ought, but the Spirit himself intercedes for us with sighs too deep for words.

—Romans 8:26

We don't know how to pray. If our praying is for an audience we can become polished and professional. But when our praying is addressed to God we are all amateurs. The evidence in the Bible is impressive. The disciples asked Jesus, "Teach us to pray." They didn't know how. They were amateurs. The most frequent lesson Jesus gave regarding prayer was be persistent. It is hard work, so keep at it. It is not easy, so hang in there. And the most complete picture we have of Jesus praying is in the Garden of Gethsemane, where he is alone, working, struggling, imploring, waiting. So what makes you think prayer will be easy? If you are praying to be heard by an audience, you can polish it, practice it, and be eloquent. But if you are praying to be heard by God, you may not know what to say.

I attended a seminar many years ago led by a famous minister. He had left the parish ministry and had started an institute for church renewal, the main thrust of which was to get the church to examine the twentieth-century world as it really is and find ways of communicating the gospel that will speak to that real world. He was not without controversy in what he did, and I personally found much with which to disagree. But he had an honesty about him that was admirable, and he was without hypocrisy. As a result he often shocked people who expected that religious people, especially ministers, conform to a certain pattern of behavior. He taught me a lesson about prayer that I'll never forget, and he did it without praying at all.

We had come to the end of a session. It was time to close with prayer and the leader asked him to deliver it. So we all stood up and waited—but there was only silence. For the longest time there was just silence, so that I wondered if he had heard the man ask him to dismiss us with a prayer. I looked up at him and saw he was obviously very uncomfortable, shifting his weight back and forth, struggling. It was not that he couldn't speak in public. He was an eloquent and dramatic speaker, and he could talk for hours without stopping. But he was tongue-tied now. He finally said, "I'm sorry. I cannot pray now."

It was an eloquent testimony that authentic prayer is often hard work. When you address your prayer to an audience, you can be professional about it and polish it. But when your prayer is addressed to God, you are always an amateur. So if you say you don't know how to pray, you have a friend in Paul. He makes the same confession right there for the whole world to see.

Then Paul applies his emphasis on the graceful initiative of God in our lives to the subject of prayer and says that prayer is not really our doing anyway. You desire to pray because God is already at work in you. God is not just the one who hears your prayer. God is the one who prompts it. You pray because God wants you to seek him. You would not be searching for God if God had not already found you.

So, Paul says, throw anything up there. Stumble, use bad grammar, have long embarrassing pauses, split your infinitives and even dangle your participles. It doesn't matter. Just groan, or sigh, if that's all you can do. Because God's hearing your prayer does not depend on your eloquence but on his grace, which already is at work in your life.

Paul couldn't get over that amazing grace. He keeps coming back to it. We are saved by God's grace and not by our own efforts. We don't know how to save ourselves by our own efforts, so God sent Jesus. We don't know how to pray by our own efforts, so God sent the Holy Spirit to intercede for us with sighs too deep for words.

So don't worry about the effort or its eloquence. Don't worry about conforming to the pattern of what others think is a proper prayer. Throw anything up there, trusting that because of God's grace it will be heard and understood.

An old Jewish legend tells about a little farm boy who had been left an orphan at an early age and was unable to read. But he had inherited a large, heavy prayer book from his parents. On the Day of Atonement he brought the prayer book into the synagogue and laid it on the desk. He then cried out, "Lord of Creation, I do not know how to pray. I do not know what to say. So I give you the entire prayer book."

In the same village there was an old man who on the Day of Atonement overslept and missed the service. That meant that the prayers offered did not include him. Not knowing how to pray by himself, he devised this plan. He repeated the letters of the alphabet over and over and asked God to arrange them into the words of an appropriate prayer. Both prayers were acceptable because of the faith of those who offered them.

Our prayers do not depend on our eloquence but on God's grace. If we do not know how to pray, the Spirit intercedes for us.

You ought to put this poem by Stephen Crane in the place where you do your prayers.

> There was a man with tongue of wood
> Who essayed to sing,
> And in truth it was lamentable.
> But there was one who heard
> The clip-clapper of this tongue of wood
> And knew what the man
> Wished to sing,
> And with that the singer was content.

After he talks about the Spirit interceding in our prayers, Paul gets even more steamed up about grace. He is going to say things that Christians will struggle to understand for two thousand years, and many will misread him. But if you remember that in these verses he is building a rhapsody on the theme of grace, you will not only understand, but marvel at what he is saying.

He says, God works for good in everything with those who love God and are called to his purpose. Look at Paul's argument. He has said we don't know how to save ourselves by our own efforts so God sent Jesus. Then, we don't know how to pray by our own efforts, so God sent the Spirit to intercede for us. And now, we don't know how to arrange our lives so that good can come out of our mistakes and failures, so God surrounds our lives with providence, and works for good in everything that happens to us.

Then Paul takes one even more daring step. He reasons that if in everything God works for good, then our life begins, continues, and ends with grace.

> For those whom he foreknew he also predestined to be conformed to the image of his Son. . . . And those whom he predestined he also called; and those whom he called he also justified; and those whom he justified he also glorified.
>
> —Romans 8:29–30

When Paul gets going on grace you can't stop him. Grace is everywhere.

And that got Paul in trouble. For along came those with smaller minds and less imagination to make ''predestination'' into a law. Paul meant it to be a rhapsody on grace. They turned it into a damnable law that read, The way you are now is the way God intended you to be and you aren't going to be anything else. John Wesley called the ''law'' of predestination ''pernicious,'' and he fought against it all his life. Wesley knew that those old crusty Calvinists were misreading Paul. What Paul was saying is that our life is created by grace, guided by grace, redeemed by grace, and in the end, glorified by grace. Grace is everywhere.

That is Paul's theme, and occasionally he breaks out into rhapsody and says things such as we are even predestined for goodness. We can't escape it if we open our hearts to it. In everything God works for good with those who love him. You start speculating on the possibilities of that and you have to come out with something like predestination. Not the Calvinistic kind. The kind the psalmist talked about.

> O Lord, thou hast searched me and known me!
> Thou knowest when I sit down and when I rise up;
>   thou discernest my thoughts from afar.
> Thou searchest out my path and my lying down,
>   and art acquainted with all my ways.

Even before a word is on my tongue,
  lo, O Lord, thou knowest it altogether.
Thou dost beset me behind and before,
  and layest thy hand upon me.
Such knowledge is too wonderful for me;
  it is high, I cannot attain it.

Whither shall I go from thy Spirit?
  Or whither shall I flee from thy presence?
If I ascend to heaven, thou art there!
  If I make my bed in Sheol, thou art there!
If I take the wings of the morning
  and dwell in the uttermost parts of the sea,
even there thy hand shall lead me,
  and thy right hand shall hold me.
If I say, "Let only darkness cover me,
  and the light about me be night,"
even the darkness is not dark to thee,
  the night is as bright as the day;
  for darkness is as light with thee.
                              —Psalm 139:1–12

That is what Paul is saying. Predestination does not mean we are trapped in some kind of fate. It means we are never trapped. It means that in everything God works for good with those who love God.

My father-in-law is a consummate fisherman. He was visiting us in San Diego when the word came that the yellow fin tuna had moved in close and the boats were bringing back hundreds of them. Yellow fin tuna are something to behold and a match for any fisherman. So we went out, about fifty miles eventually, and got skunked. We couldn't find a yellow fin anywhere.

As we were coming in we sailed right into a school of porpoise, jumping and frolicking over what must have been several miles of sea. There were hundreds of them. As soon as they spotted the boat, they challenged us to a race, speeding along the bow of our boat at about fourteen knots. It was beautiful to see their effortless grace, their playful exuberance, their joy in the life God created for them.

I wish I could say that seeing those porpoise made up for not catching any fish, but I'd be lying. But it did remind me of a description of porpoise written by Jacques Cousteau. He pointed out that when a baby porpoise is born, other porpoise will lift the freshly born youngster to the surface for its first breath. Cousteau wrote that many tales have been reported of shipwrecked sailors struggling in the water. Just as their strength was almost gone, the strong, sleek body of a porpoise would instinctively buoy them up. Some stories report that the porpoise will even escort them to shallow water and safety. As I leaned over the bow of our boat and watched the race, I thought of Cousteau's message.

And then I remembered the stories I have heard others tell, not of porpoise, but of friends, who came unexpectedly to lift them in a time of sorrow. And of others who went to someone in their loneliness and communicated that they understood. And of still others who thought they were sinking under the weight of a heavy burden, but who somehow found strength they did not know they had.

They could all testify, as John Newton did in the song "Amazing Grace,"

> Through many dangers, toils, and snares,
> I have already come;
> 'Tis grace hath brought me safe thus far,
> And grace will lead me home.

Grace is everywhere. "God works for good with those who love him, who are called according to his purpose."

V

The Providence
of God

I consider that the sufferings of this present time are not worth comparing with the glory that is to be revealed to us. For the creation waits with eager longing for the revealing of the sons of God; for the creation was subjected to futility, not of its own will but by the will of him who subjected it in hope; because the creation itself will be set free from its bondage to decay and obtain the glorious liberty of the children of God.

We know that the whole creation has been groaning in travail together until now; and not only the creation, but we ourselves, who have the first fruits of the Spirit, groan inwardly as we wait for adoption as sons, the redemption of our bodies. For in this hope we were saved. Now hope that is seen is not hope. For who hopes for what he sees? But if we hope for what we do not see, we wait for it with patience.

—Romans 8:18–25

9

Why Murphy Is Right

"Murphy's Law" reads, "Anything that can go wrong, will go wrong." Murphy has inspired other laws describing those areas of life where forces seem to work against us.

There are the laws that govern bureaucracies. "Somewhere right now a committee is deciding your future, and you weren't invited." "When all is said and done, more will be said than done." Anyone who has had to stand in line at a government office knows, "The other line always moves faster."

There are laws describing the demonic forces set in motion whenever you attempt home repairs. "If you tinker with something long enough, it will eventually break." "Every job takes more time than you have." The law always at work when I try to fix anything says, "Every object will fall so as to do the most damage."

And there are those that underscore the unfairness and absurdity of life. J. Paul Getty's famous line, "The meek shall inherit the earth, but not its mineral rights." Or, "Negative expectations yield negative results. Positive expectations yield negative results." "Whatever hits the fan won't be distributed evenly." And Woody Allen's Law, his revision of the "Peaceable Kingdom" passage from Isaiah, "The lion and the calf shall lie down together but the calf won't get much sleep."

Murphy's Law points to one of the deepest mysteries of life;

there seems to be something working against our dreams, our hopes, and our best efforts. Philosopher Miguel de Unamuno called this the tragic sense of life.

Have you ever had the experience of gathering with friends for a reunion? You knew some before they were married, watched their children grow up, partied with them, wept with them. Now you gather in the summertime for a reunion. If you were to list all the tragedies that have befallen the people in that group, that small circle of friends, they would be Jobean in dimension.

Martin Marty and his wife attended such a reunion of friends. He wrote that while they were driving home the next morning they compared notes, listing all the hurt their friends had endured. Two of the couples were there to introduce new partners, replacing those lost in death. Another man came alone; he had to leave his youngish wife in a nursing home. Parents were there who had lost children. Two families had endured heartache and trauma because of what had happened to their children. Another woman was there who had a debilitating disease. A man's wife and two sons were killed in one fell swoop.

We could share similar experiences of friends and family whose pain and hurt don't make sense. When we see the suffering we say it's not right. It is not the way things should be. There is something terribly wrong, deep down in the world, that makes that kind of thing happen.

In this passage Paul speaks of that mysterious presence of evil in the world.

> We know that the whole creation has been groaning in travail together until now; and not only the creation, but we ourselves, who have the first fruits of the Spirit, groan inwardly as we wait for adoption as sons, the redemption of our bodies
>
> —Romans 8:22–23

First, he envisions a unity in all creation. The whole creation groans in travail together. Instead of a static, fixed, and completed world, Paul uses an image of a world growing, moving, evolving, groaning together toward its goal. A unity of creation. In the nineteenth verse of this same chapter, he says, "All of creation waits with eager longing (TEV).

What a marvelous picture of creation. We are in this together, not just you and me, not just the human community, but all of creation together.

Many jokes have been made about people talking to plants, but studies with sophisticated equipment such as Kirlian photography and galvanometers indicate that evidently there is a response in plants to human influence. If so, that old idea that some people have a green thumb is not too far off. Experiments have indicated that some people have fields of energy, auras, that have a positive influence on the growth of plants.

We recognize the same phenomenon in some human beings who seem to have a special rapport with wild animals. Some apparently are able actually to communicate with them, like St. Francis, who preached to the birds. Francis addressed all creation, rocks and trees, beetles and lizards, the sun and moon, as his brothers and sisters.

One of the concerns of theoretical science is to explore the full meaning of living in a universe. They take the meaning of universe, literally, and try to find out why it is that things so dissimilar apparently operate by the same laws—not just within each level of creation, but between human life and inanimate matter, and between matter here on earth and all the other bodies in the universe. As Sir James Jeans said many years ago, "Every time a child throws his rattle out of the crib, it affects the motion of the stars in the heavens."

We live in a universe. In Latin, *universe* means turning, or moving, together. All creation groaning in travail, moving toward a goal, waiting for the final redemption of life.

Secondly, Paul's vision instructs us to have a healthy realism about this world. If the world is still moving, growing, and groaning, don't expect to have an easy time of it. Life can be hard. Don't expect to get up every morning singing, "Oh, what a beautiful morning . . . everything's going my way," because some day things are going to go against you.

The story is told that one day Queen Victoria, riding in her royal yacht on the Irish Sea, came into one of those storms that arise so quickly on that impetuous sea. The storm tossed and buffeted the ship as if it were a toy. When they finally made it safely to port, Queen Victoria said to her doctor, who was in attendance, "Go up at once, Sir James, and give the admiral my compliments and tell him the thing must not occur again."

There are storms we can't control. They just happen, and there isn't anything we can do about them except ride them out. We would like to believe differently. We would like to believe that the bad things in this life persist because we haven't found the right attitude to master them, or the right technique to control them. We would like to believe that we could manage our feelings if only we could find the right formula, or solve society's problems if we could find the right social policy. We would like to believe that the problem is that we have a few quirks that need adjustment.

Well, we all have a few quirks that we could adjust and live happier lives. A lot of people do stupid things and suffer misery as a result. We can improve our lives, that is true.

But there is also that tragic element of life—that you can't do anything about—that comes upon us not because we are not what we are supposed to be, but because the creation is not yet the way it is supposed to be. By virtue of the fact that we are part of the creation, we will participate in its travail.

That is how I understand natural disasters and cataclysmic disease that come to human life. We suffer them not because we aren't the way we are supposed to be. They happen because the creation is not yet the way God wants it to be.

A Los Angeles newspaper editorial deplored the tragic situation in a South American country under an unusually brutal dictatorship. The editor lamented the fact that other countries of the world would not speak out because they depended on this country's exports of strategic raw materials. The editor wrote, "If this were truly a decent and sane world . . ." and then prescribed what should happen. But that is the problem. Sometimes the world is decent and sane, but other times it is mad and inhumane. Christians who are committed to eliminate poverty, stop injustice, and put an end to war had better be prepared for qualified success. We had better be realistic about the results of our efforts. The world is not yet the way God wants it to be. It is still growing. As the mayor of Dublin put it at a memorial service for John Kennedy, "What's the good of being Irish, if you do not know that someday the world will rise up and break your heart?"

The third lesson is that most suffering has no answer. We want there to be an answer. We want there to be a simple answer for all the suffering in this world. We read the Bible as if it described a neat, tidy, static, stable world in which everything has a reason. The world the Bible actually describes is a moving, growing, groaning world in which things wait patiently—all things—for answers.

The Book of Job poignantly records the groaning of creation and the desperate longing for answers that do not come. That is why we talk about the patience of Job. He waits for answers that do not come. Jesus doesn't give us easy answers either, not on this subject. Remember that tragic scene in the Gospel of John when his friend Lazarus dies. Lazarus' sisters ask for Jesus but he does not come. When he finally arrives, the sisters say, "If you had been here."

The scene is drawn this way to raise the questions we would ask God. The Gospel of John takes seriously Jesus' words, "He who has seen me has seen the Father" (John 14:9). So John asks Jesus, "Why don't you do something? Why did he have to die? Where were you when we needed you?" (author's paraphrase). And there are no answers, except, John says, Jesus wept, and then raised Lazarus from the dead, which, John says, was his last and greatest sign.

No answers. Only signs we are to trust. The sign that God knows us, knows the hurt we feel, and weeps with us. And the sign that God is able to bring new life out of suffering. No answers, but deeds we are to remember and trust. God cries, and God resurrects.

In the weeks following Lincoln's assassination there were

many sermons setting forth reasons for the tragedy. Somebody studied those sermons and concluded that all but one offered a reason for the tragedy. That one exception was the sermon preached by Dr. Gurley, the minister of the Presbyterian church Lincoln attended when he worshiped publicly. Gurley was the only minister who knew Lincoln well, and one of the few ministers Lincoln liked. In that sermon Gurley saw no reason for this "mysterious and most afflicting visitation." But, he said, he would wait, with strong faith that God would explain sometime in the future.

We are not given answers. Not yet. We are given signs to trust—signs that God shares in our suffering and is able to bring new life out of our suffering.

After describing the tragic dimension in life, Paul concludes with these words. "I consider that the sufferings of this present time are not worth comparing with the glory that is to be revealed to us" (Rom. 8:18).

So Christians are not only realistic, they are optimistic. Christians are realists because they have no illusions about life. They know all about the tragic dimension. But they are optimistic because they know that the sufferings of the present time can be used by God to bring about another time.

Go back to the party of the old friends, the ones who have experienced enough of life to know its tragic dimension. What do they do? They keep on going. And they make their sufferings count. Their sufferings don't remind them of the past so much as they give them a keener appreciation of the joy of the present. They don't feel sorry for themselves so much as they feel for others. They keep going, and they get involved. Having been through the travail themselves, they can appreciate what other people are going through. They know that the world can break your heart, but they also know they can rely on God's promises. So they live with hope, and wait with eager expectation for the renewal of life.

This passage takes on even more meaning when we realize that the image of groaning and travail is the image the Bible uses for childbirth. The metaphor reveals that the travail of life is the pain God uses to bring about new life. Romans is not the only place where the metaphor is used. In the last chapter of the Book of Isaiah, the prophet speaks of Israel, the nation, being in travail, suffering immensely. God speaks. "Shall I bring to the birth and not cause to bring forth?" (Isa. 66:9).

Those who live by faith that God keeps promises believe that the suffering of this life is like the labor of a woman in childbirth, and out of it will come a joy, a new life, grander than you could ever imagine. That is why Paul sings, "I consider that the sufferings of this present time are not worth comparing with the glory that is to be revealed to us" (Rom. 8:18).

What then shall we say to this? If God is for us, who is against us? He who did not spare his own Son but gave him up for us all, will he not also give us all things with him? Who shall bring any charge against God's elect? It is God who justifies; who is to condemn? Is it Christ Jesus, who died, yes, who was raised from the dead, who is at the right hand of God, who indeed intercedes for us? Who shall separate us from the love of Christ? Shall tribulation, or distress, or persecution, or famine, or nakedness, or peril, or sword? As it is written,

"For thy sake we are being killed all the day long;
we are regarded as sheep to be slaughtered."

No, in all things we are more than conquerors through him who loved us. For I am sure that neither death, nor life, nor angels, nor principalities, nor things present, nor things to come, nor powers, nor height, nor depth, nor anything else in all creation, will be able to separate us from the love of God in Christ Jesus our Lord.

—Romans 8:31–39

10

More Than Conquerors

In the movie *Star Wars,* the old desert nomad, Ben Kenobi, says to Luke, the young idealist: "These are dark times. The days when the Empire rules."

The Empire is a galactic empire, and it rules with awesome technological power and efficiency. The Galactic Empire is evil projected to a cosmic scale.

Opposing this evil empire is a small band of humans who have fled to a remote planet with earth-like vegetation to organize resistance to the Galactic Empire. They are outnumbered and overpowered, but they win. They don't really win, because there must be enough left of the Galactic Empire to make another movie, but for all intents and purposes they win.

They conquer the evil empire not because they possess superior armaments, vaster resources, or larger armies. They succeed because they are supported by the spiritual reality called "The Force." The Force, though invisible, is the strongest power in the universe, and it is on their side. Old Ben Kenobi, who has such love that he lays down his life for his friends, returns to Luke as a spiritual presence and says, "Use the Force, Luke, trust me, and use the Force."

Nearly two thousand years ago in this galaxy and on this planet a small band of Christians gathered together in fear of another empire, this one called the Roman Empire. They saw that empire as evil projected to a cosmic scale. The Book of Revelation describes the Roman Empire as an earthly manifestation of a cosmic evil. What chance did this small band of faithful people have against a power that had connections with the supernatural, evil forces of the universe? To the Ephesians, Paul wrote, "For we are not contending against flesh and blood, but against the principalities, against the powers, against the world rulers of this present darkness, against the spiritual hosts of wickedness in heavenly places" (Eph. 6:12). That is how they described Rome. What could they do against such a power? They would have been content simply to survive. Paul says to them, "You are going to conquer."

There are times when we feel helpless. Helplessness is the feeling that there are powers greater than ours that control our destiny. Paul lists these powers, some we know and some are strange to us.

First, "death," the limit on all of our lives.

Then he mentions "life," meaning that experience that prompts us to say, "Well, that's just life." The capricious way that life throws things in our path.

Next, "things present," the things we can see and fear are going to overwhelm us.

And "things to come," the things we fear because we cannot see them.

All these powers are familiar to us—death, life, things present, and things to come.

But then he mentions things that are strange to us, such as "angels," and "principalities," and "height" and "depth." In those days they believed there were superhuman beings, not unlike Darth Vader, that archvillain in Star Wars, who dwelt in the lower stories of heaven and who controlled the events on earth. They were called "angels" and "principalities." They were the reason earthquakes leveled cities, plagues swept across nations, volcanoes erupted, and men went to war. Principalities, and power, and angels, they were called, and in the face of them human beings could do nothing.

Then the strange reference to "height" and "depth," astrological terms. When a star is in its height, its influence over your life is supposed to be the greatest. At its depth, its lowest point in the heavens, its power over you is the least. The combination of the two, an evil star at its height and your "lucky" star at its depth, would spell disaster for you. When that configuration came into the heavens, you were helpless. There was nothing you could do.

Paul tells these embattled Christians that there is a force now stronger than any of these powers. These powers may seem to determine your life, but they do not. God is in control, the God who has revealed the power which created you by grace, redeemed you by grace, interceded for you in your prayers by grace, and who, in the end, will welcome you home by grace.

You and I may have trouble with Paul's "principalities and powers." We may consider ourselves too sophisticated to think of the world in terms of a cataclysmic battle between the forces of evil and the forces of good. But we still know what it means to be given a destiny in this life. Otherwise we might not have chosen, if we had been consulted, our looks, or our temperament, or even our names.

I remember a cartoon showing a meek-looking man talking to a beautiful woman at a party. He says, "My father named me Harley Davidson after his motorcycle." That was his fate. He had to live with that name the rest of his life.

We are not only given our names by our parents, but our looks, our temperament, our health, and to a large extent, I am told, our intelligence. To that degree at least our parents determine our fate in this life.

Our environment, especially in childhood, shapes our fate. In spite of some notable exceptions, if you are born into a home of poverty and despair, you start life behind those who are born into more favorable circumstances. Those who have a secure and privileged childhood are born under a "lucky star." They had nothing to do with it. It was just good fortune.

Some physical handicaps are given to us as if there were some fate determining our lives. I read about a boy permanently handicapped, his frail body damaged at birth because the umbilical cord wrapped around his neck when he was born. The doctor didn't know it. In that case there was nothing anybody could do. They were helpless. The boy had been given a fate he did not deserve, and should not have had, but he could do nothing about it.

And there are those events that come to us out of nowhere. Someone has to drop out of life, shattered emotionally. We ask, Why? Is it because of some stress or because of a genetic weakness? Is it physiological or emotional? We ask why especially when it happens to us, or someone we love. We want to know because knowledge will enable us to control that power that seems to control us. But there is no answer.

The message of Paul comes to us as it did to those first Christians: There is only one power greater than you, and that power is God, your Creator, and God already has shown through Jesus that God is for you and not against you. And now God has shown you through the Spirit in the church that God supports you and sustains you in your struggles. So trust God. Use the power. And you will become more than conqueror through him who loves us. For if God is for us, Who can be against us?

The eighth chapter of Romans is one of the peaks of biblical literature, a watershed dividing history. I don't know if Paul was aware of what he was doing when he wrote this letter. I doubt that he was, because artists, prophets, and apostles—those who are inspired, who open their talents to God's Spirit—often are unaware of the full significance of what they are creating. They often are the instruments of something greater than they could ever imagine.

The fact is that because of this announcement, "If God is for us, who is against us," there was a new heaven and a new earth. The powers people believed were against us were driven out of heaven, and the demons they feared were driven off the earth.

Before Christ, people believed supernatural powers in the heavens and on the earth determined their destiny. But after Paul, all gods, forces, astrologies, demons—the whole spooky business—was relegated to superstition. Now you can live in a world that is friendly and hospitable. Now you can become conqueror over whatever it is that seems to threaten your life, even though that power seems greater than your power. Now there is a new power from which nothing else in all creation can separate us. So use the power, Paul tells the Romans, and become more than conqueror.

There is an old theological debate over whether we determine our lives or whether God determines them for us. Paul resolves the conflict by saying God works through us. If we don't act, God can't. If we don't try to conquer, God can't give us the victory. If we don't use the power, it's not there.

Donald Baillie, the great Scottish theologian who authored *God Was in Christ,* called this "the paradox of Grace." It is a marvelous term, the experience of doing something and then, in retrospect, seeing that you had help. Paul put it this way to the Corinthians, "I worked harder than any of them, though it was not I, but the grace of God which is with me" (1 Cor. 15:10). That is the paradox of grace. I did it, but with God's grace.

The Jews have a legend which says that when the Hebrews escaped from Egypt and came to the Red Sea, it seemed they were trapped. There was the great expanse of the water in front of them, the horde of Pharaoh's army bearing down behind them. And nothing happened until the first Hebrew stepped into the water. Then the sea parted.

That is the way it will be for you. Nothing will happen until you take the first step. And then because you do, God can. So for all practical purposes, don't wait around for God to take the initiative. He probably won't do it. Without God we cannot, that's true. But it is also true to say without you God won't.

One of the great moments in sports occurred when the New York Jets met the Baltimore Colts in the 1969 Super Bowl. Nobody expected that the Jets would have a chance. The Jets represented that weak league, the American, against the mighty National Football League and their representative, the Baltimore Colts, led by the legendary Johnny Unitas. It was like David going against Goliath, or like Luke Skywalker going against Darth Vader in "Star Wars."

John Dockery, a member of that 1969 Jets team, described what happened during that game in Florida. "It was a moment late in the third quarter when I looked up at the scoreboard and it flashed through my mind like a bolt of lightning, 'We're going to win! My God, we're actually going to win!' "

Paul ended this part of his message with the announcement, "We're going to win." We will still have to fight and struggle and endure and be patient, but we are going to win. If God is for us, who is against us?" (Rom. 8:31).

VI

The Church
in the World

Lest you be wise in your own conceits, I want you to understand this mystery, brethren: a hardening has come upon part of Israel, until the full number of the Gentiles come in, and so all Israel will be saved; as it is written,

> *"The Deliverer will come from Zion,*
> *he will banish ungodliness from Jacob";*
> *"and this will be my covenant with them*
> *when I take away their sins."*

As regards the gospel they are enemies of God, for your sake; but as regards election they are beloved for the sake of their forefathers. For the gifts and the call of God are irrevocable. Just as you were once disobedient to God but now have received mercy because of their disobedience, so they have now been disobedient in order that by the mercy shown to you they also may receive mercy. For God has consigned all men to disobedience, that he may have mercy upon all.

—Romans 11:25–32

11

_x_ **How Odd of God**

Christianity makes an absolute claim about Jesus. We don't say that Jesus was just a very good man. We don't even say he was a very, very good man. We say that Jesus was the Son of God.

In his second letter to the Corinthians Paul says, "God was in Christ reconciling the world to himself . . . and entrusting to us the ministry of reconciliation" (2 Cor. 5:19). Christians have that imperative to spread the Word about what has happened to the world. We also have the command of Jesus himself, "Go therefore and make disciples of all nations, baptizing them in the name of the Father and the Son and the Holy Spirit" (Matt. 28:19). There is an imperative to spread the Word.

But there is also a caution to do it humbly. You don't know enough about another person to prescribe their salvation for them. And you don't know enough about God to predict how God is going to work in somebody's life. So be humble in what you think you know about God and what you think you can do for somebody else.

The caution is prompted by what is called the mystery of God. The incomparable poetry of Job captures it.

> He stretches out the north over the void,
>   and hangs the earth upon nothing.
> He binds up the waters in his thick clouds,
>   and the cloud is not rent under them.

He has described a circle upon the face of
the waters
at the boundary between light and darkness.

Lo, these are but the outskirts of his ways;
and how small a whisper do we hear of him!
Job 26: 7–8,10,12*a*

Paul marvels at the mystery that accompanies God's revelation, "O the depth of the riches and wisdom and knowledge of God! How unsearchable are his judgments and how inscrutable his ways!" (Rom. 11:33).

Knowledge of the mystery of God should encourage humility in the religious. We only see the outskirts of God's way. We don't see everything that God is going to do in this world, nor do we hear everything God has to say. We hear only the whisper that God has spoken to us.

There are several kinds of mysteries in that life. The mysteries will disappear when we gain more knowledge, or grow up, or gain more experience. A little boy wonders why anybody would ever want to kiss a girl. It is a mystery to him. But one day he will understand. There are those stories we call mystery stories because we don't know what is going to happen until we read to that point in the story where the evidence is given that enables the plot to make sense. When we gain insight the mystery disappears. There are mysteries which are solved with knowledge.

But there are also mysteries which are enhanced by knowledge. The more you know, the greater the mystery. Immature science talks about the laws of the universe. Mature science talks about the mystery of the universe. More knowledge in science does not erase mystery from the world, it heightens it. Huston Smith said, "The larger the island of knowledge the longer the shoreline of wonder."

That is especially true of human beings. Those people who don't know somebody very well can make conclusive judgments about what that person is like. But those who really know the person realize how complex that person really is. The greater the knowledge the more complex we see a person to be.

If that is true of human beings, how much more is it true of God? God is not a mystery that more knowledge will explain. The more God reveals to us, the more wonderful God is to us. We worship God, Frederick Buechner said in *Wishful Thinking,* because you can never nail God down. "Even on Christ the nails proved ultimately ineffective." The more God reveals to us, the more mysterious God becomes. More knowledge about God does not lead to more information about God. It leads to worship. God's judgments are unsearchable and God's ways are inscrutable.

Humility about our knowledge of God will result in some practical consequences in the way we relate to others. Sensitive Christians worry about a spouse, or a son or daughter, who does not believe the way they do. Sometimes we feel because one doesn't believe what we were taught is the truth, that person must be in error, or worse, they have slipped away from the grace of God.

But the mystery of God leads us to acknowledge that God is larger than any of our beliefs. Because God speaks to us through what we believe, does not mean God cannot speak to others through what they believe. That is hard for me to accept sometimes. I see all the ridiculous things that people believe, and it seems impossible that what they believe could ever lead them to God.

And that is where Paul's emphasis on God's grace in our redemption provides another revolutionary insight. If God has come to us, our beliefs don't have to lead us to God. In fact no belief captures God. Beliefs are not something you pile up, one on top of another, until you climb high enough to shake hands with God. No matter how high we stack our beliefs they will never reach God. Beliefs are not our way of reaching God, but one of the means God can use to come to us. It is a mystery, I grant you, but God can come to me, and to those who disagree with me.

Luther was famous for his iconoclastic statements. But he was especially so, although he was probably right, when he said, "Nobody in this life is nearer to God than those who hate and deny him." He meant that those who claim to be agnostic, or even atheist, take God seriously, and often those who appear to be religious because they believe a lot of things about God, may be the farthest away from him. And besides, often what the non-believer is rejecting is not God, but somebody's beliefs about God.

If we are worried about a person who says he is an agnostic or even an atheist, we need to know that person is not far from God. The real question is not, Do we believe in God? but Does God believe in us? And the answer of the gospel is yes. God's acceptance of us is not based on our believing in God, but on God's grace toward us.

Kosuge Koyama is a Japanese Christian theologian who calls for humility on the part of Christians in approaching those who believe differently than we do. He says that the tragedy, and often the failure, of Christian evangelism has been that it has assumed the stance of superiority. According to the historical atlas of the world's religions, there are 1,425,000,000 people who adhere to major religions other than Christianity.

Koyama says that if we believe Jesus Christ died for those millions of people, then we must be careful what we say about them. He adds that we should approach them with humility and respect, as Jesus, who died for them, would approach them with love and understanding, and see them as children of God.

Paul makes the statement about God's inscrutable ways at the conclusion of three long chapters in which he discusses the salvation of the Jews. He spends more time on that question than he does anything else. Chapters 9, 10, and 11, three lengthy chapters, are devoted to this one subject. It obviously was a question he wrestled with for a long time, one the Roman Church was faced with, and a question Christians have not dealt with honestly for two thousand years. We must confess that much of our relationship with Judaism has been based on anti-Semitism.

Paul counsels humility. "Lest you be wise in your own conceits, I want you to understand this mystery, brethren" (Rom. 11:25). In spite of what has happened, God has not rejected the Jews. They are God's children by birth. We Christians are sons and daughters of God by adoption. But they are God's children by birth. The Jews are our older brothers and sisters, the elders in the family of God. Then Paul changes the analogy and says, "They are the tree. We are the branches." And besides that, we are grafted on. They got the original invitation to the party. We crashed it. They have been working in the vineyard for years. We are the migrant workers who were hired in the last hours through the grace of God.

So be humble, Paul says. The Jews are something special and they always will be. They were chosen to be God's people and God will never reject them.

At the heart of God's mystery is grace. That is what always confounds us, the way God deals with us. Christians are justified by grace, the Jews were chosen by it. They didn't have anything to do with it. For a while they thought that being chosen revealed something wonderful about their Jewishness, but it didn't. It revealed something wonderful about God.

And when God makes a promise, he never breaks it—just as the promise to Abraham back there, four thousand years ago now, that Abraham's descendants would be the chosen people. Therefore, Paul says, they won't ever be anything else. To believe otherwise is to say God doesn't keep his promise. If you can't believe anything else, you had better believe that, God keeps his promises. Otherwise, we are left with chaos.

"Lest you be wise in your own conceits," Paul admonishes us, "I want you to understand this mystery" (Rom. 11:25). The Jews are our older brothers and sisters. God has chosen to open the promise of salvation to everybody—to the Greeks, the Romans, the Africans, the Asians, the Europeans—so that the whole blooming creation can now come into the family of God. The Jews will always have a special place in that family; and we, as Christians, ought to have a humility appropriate to that fact.

Le Chambon-Feugerolles is a village in the southern mountains of France. It is Huguenot country down there. Huguenots are French protestants who suffered some persecution after the reformation in Catholic-dominated France and fled for refuge to villages in the French Alps.

During World War II, the pastor of the church in Le Chambon

was André Trocme who, like many Huguenots, was a pacifist. They would not fight against the Nazis nor take up arms against the Vichy government. But neither would they cooperate. Their nonviolent resistance was such a befuddlement to the Germans that they virtually left them alone. As a result, the Huguenot villages became perfect hiding places for Jewish refugees.

Nobody knows how many Jews were smuggled into those towns, but apparently thousands of Jewish lives were spared because people like André Trocme hid them in their homes. Most of the time the Huguenot villages were secure enough for the refugees to walk freely about the town. One day a refugee was sent by her host to a farm outside the village to buy some eggs. When she got to the kitchen of the farm house she was invited in by the farmer's wife, who then stared at her and asked, "You . . . you are Jewish?" The Jewish woman, who had been tortured in Germany because of her Jewishness, stepped back, trembling. The farm woman ran to the stairs. The Jewish woman prepared to bolt, certain the woman was going to betray her. "Look, look, my family!" the farmer's wife called. Then as her family walked into the kitchen, she stood proudly next to the frightened woman, and said, "We have in our house now a representative of the Chosen People."

Humility becomes a Christian. Paul says, "Lest you become conceited I am going to tell you something. The Jews are the honored elder brothers and sisters. They are living proof among us that God's promise is always kept."

I appeal to you therefore, brethren, by the mercies of God, to present your bodies as a living sacrifice, holy and acceptable to God, which is your spiritual worship. Do not be conformed to this world but be transformed by the renewal of your mind, that you may prove what is the will of God, what is good and acceptable and perfect.

For by the grace given to me I bid every one among you not to think of himself more highly than he ought to think, but to think with sober judgment, each according to the measure of faith which God has assigned him.

Bless those who persecute you; bless and do not curse them. Rejoice with those who rejoice, weep with those who weep. Live in harmony with one another; do not be haughty, but associate with the lowly; never be conceited. Repay no one evil for evil, but take thought for what is noble in the sight of all. If possible, so far as it depends upon you, live peaceably with all. Beloved, never avenge yourselves, but leave it to the wrath of God; for it is written, "Vengeance is mine, I will repay, says the Lord." No, "if your enemy is hungry, feed him; if he is thirsty, give him drink; for by so doing you will heap burning coals upon his head." Do not be overcome by evil, but overcome evil with good.

—Romans 12:1–3, 14–21

12

⨯ Be a Little Crazy
———❧⚓☙———

Dostoyevsky analyzed what was wrong in the society of Imperial Russia. His diagnosis could have been written for our time.

With our universal indifference to the sublime aims of life, perhaps in some strata of our society, the family is already in a state of decomposition. It is clear that our young generation is destined to seek ideals for itself. . . . But . . . this abandonment of youth to their own resources—this is what is dreadful. . . . Our youth is so placed that absolutely nowhere does it find advice as to the loftiest meaning of life. From our brainy people and generally, from their leaders, youth . . . can borrow merely a rather satirical view, but nothing positive, *i.e.*, in what to believe, what should be respected and adored, and what should be sought; and yet all of this is so needed. . . .

Someone to hold to the loftiest aims of life—it was needed then and it is needed now.

Madeleine L'Engle talked about contemporary literature. She once said, "I am bored stiff with anti-heroes. I want to read somebody who is going to make me feel like I can do more, not that I am stuck with being less."

There is a Christian way of living in this world. That seems so elementary that it need not even be spoken; but, in fact, it will come as news to many people, even to some inside the church, who think that morality is determined by public opinion. A poll is taken to ask what everybody thinks about sexual morality, family life, business ethics, or social policy, and the results become the new morality. Nobody asks the qualitative questions. Is it right? Is it noble? Is it helpful? It is sufficient to know that everybody is doing it. By the fact of being measured, recorded, and published, it becomes normative.

Paul holds up a different standard for the Christian. "Do not be conformed to this world but be transformed by the renewal of your mind, that you may prove what is . . . good and acceptable and perfect" (Rom. 12:2).

By conforming to the world, he means letting what is happening now determine the way you are going to live. Today everything is permissible. Society will tolerate just about anything. I don't like that, especially as an environment in which to raise my family. But I can live with it as preferable to a repressive society with a single standard of behavior forced on everyone. That kind of society has its own problems. Furthermore, in a permissive society morality has greater meaning. A decision is moral only if you have a choice between right and wrong. If you do not have a choice your deed may be innocent, but it hardly can be called moral. Finally, contrary to our fears, Christianity always has flourished in permissive societies where it offers a clear alternative for a *better* life.

The first century was a case in point. It was wide open in that Greek and Roman world. Everything was permissible. In that context Paul wrote, "Everything is permissible but not everything is good or true or beautiful or right." What distinguished a Christian in those days was that he or she lived for the nobler aims of life. You could pick them out not from some symbol they wore, nor from a bumper sticker on the back of their chariots. You could identify them by looking at the quality of their lives.

"Do not be conformed to this world but be transformed by the renewal of your mind" (Rom. 12:2a). In Greek the word for mind is *nous*. It means making critical judgments about right and wrong, using your mind to make moral choices. What is required of Christians is that they demonstrate in the quality of their living what is good and acceptable and perfect.

Even though Christians have never agreed on one style of life, they do agree that the standard for Christian behavior is not taken from the world. It is taken from Christ. The question the Christian should ask is not, "Is everybody doing it?" but, "Is it what Christ would have me do?"

The monastic movement began because some felt not conforming to the world meant you had to get out of the world. They believed that if you were really serious about being a Christian you got yourself to a monastery.

The puritan spirit emerged when not conforming was interpreted to mean you had to hate the world. There was a lot of that in the old Methodism where to be Christian was defined as being against a list of things, especially those things that were particularly enjoyable.

But neither the monastic nor the puritan way of life is necessarily biblical. The biblical model is being in the world but not conformed to it—enjoying the creation that God gives us, but responsibly as a steward.

Søren Kierkegaard gave us an illustration of what living in the world but not conforming to it looks like in his parable of "The Knight of Faith." If you see him walking down the street, he wrote, you probably couldn't distinguish him from anybody else. He doesn't look like he is the citizen of another world. He would probably be dressed in sartorial elegance, even in the Italian mode. He walks through the park on a Sunday afternoon enjoying the warmth of the sun, goes home to a nice dinner, sits by the fire, and reads the paper for news of the stock market. From the outside he will look like anybody else. But on the inside he is contemporaneous with Christ.

The Knight of Faith is unpredictable. You never know what he is going to do. Today, he may make a killing on the stock market. Tomorrow, he may give it all away with an heroic gesture of renunciation. He is unpredictable because he doesn't live by the standards of this world. He is in the world but not conformed to it.

He enjoys the world, but as a steward of the gifts of God. He lives in the world, but as a pilgrim, a citizen of another world. He is open to all things, but he stands for something. He knows that all things are permissible, but he also knows that not all things are Christian.

There is a Christian way of living in this world. We are to be transformed so we can prove what is good and acceptable and perfect. The point of this text is that our lives are to present the evidence that what we say about Christ is true. The word *prove* in this passage has the weight of a lawyer making his case. Our living must convince.

In a satirical novel about suburban life, *This Demi-Paradise* by Margaret Halsey, the neighborhood church was named St. Euphoria, its minister the Reverend Mr. Aspirin. The mission of that church was to sprinkle holy water on the *status quo,* to tell everybody everything is all right. The result was a community without guidance from a standard other than what's happening now. A member of that church asked, "How do you keep up the standards that you believe in? How do you keep from getting corrupted when *nobody* is around to symbolize the higher things?"

Christians are to present their lives as evidence of a better way of living in this world. The purpose of Christian morality is not to save your own soul. Christians don't worry about that. We know that we are saved by God's grace, not by our own works. The purpose of being moral is to witness to higher things, to what is good and acceptable and perfect.

As pretentious as it may sound, the purpose of Christian morality is to save the world—in the sense that Christ told us to be the salt of the earth, the leaven in the loaf, and the city set upon the hill so that "they (all) may see your good works and give glory to your Father who is in heaven" (Matt.5:16).

Then Paul gets specific. The world says curse those who get in your way, but Paul says bless them instead.

The world says think of yourself. Paul says rejoice with those who rejoice and weep with those who weep. Get outside of yourself for a change and feel what other people are feeling. Be a part of their rejoicing and know of their sorrow.

The world says always be with the right people, that is most important. And Paul says don't be haughty, but associate with the lowly.

The world says look after number one. Paul says don't think of yourself more highly than you ought to, and don't be conceited.

The world says get even. Paul says if your enemy is hungry, feed him; if he is thirsty, give him drink.

The world says everybody does it, so I will do it, too. Paul says don't be overcome with evil, but overcome evil with good.

By the standard of the world, the Christian way of living will appear unreasonable and foolish, and maybe a little bit crazy.

California's latest burgeoning industry is called the survival industry. It caters to those people who fear some impending, apocalyptic disaster. They sell real estate in remote areas of northern California and Oregon, caches of food and supplies to store away, and arms to defend against your neighbors who were not so prudent as to plan for the worst. The advertisements for this industry all preach the same worldly wisdom: it is only reasonable that in times such as this you would think first of yourself.

I remembered in contrast the account of an incident from the third century. Those were the days when the wealthy and powerful fled from the cities to build private villas and hire their own armies. The abandonment of the cities marked the beginning of feudal society and the dark ages.

There is a remarkable document that comes out of that third century, written by Cyprian, the bishop of Carthage. It is a book on patience addressed to the members of his church. The occasion of the book was the attack of a plague upon that city so severe that those who could left the city. That meant that the rich ran away and the poor, who had no choice, stayed. In that circumstance Cyprian wrote the church in Carthage to stay in the city—stay, even though it was in their power to leave. Stay so that they could minister to the sick, bury the dead, and bring hope to those who live in fear, Cyprian urged.

What makes this book so remarkable is that the plague came on the heels of a wave of persecution of the Christians in that city, in the course of which many were imprisoned and some killed. The temptation of the Christian community must have been to say, "What do we owe the city of Carthage after what they have done to us? The plague surely is the judgment of God upon the city." But they didn't yield to that bitterness. Instead they stayed and became the servants of those who had most recently been their persecutors.

You have to be a little crazy to live as a Christian in this world. While the wisdom of the world may destroy the place, it just may be that the foolishness of Christ will still save it.

That is why Paul writes the Romans, "Do not be conformed to this world but be transformed by the renewal of your mind, that you may prove what is the will of God, what is good and acceptable and perfect" (Rom. 12:2).

Let every person be subject to the governing authorities. For there is no authority except from God, and those that exist have been instituted by God. Therefore he who resists the authorities resists what God has appointed, and those who resist will incur judgment. For rulers are not a terror to good conduct, but to bad. Would you have no fear of him who is in authority? Then do what is good, and you will receive his approval, for he is God's servant for your good. But if you do wrong, be afraid, for he does not bear the sword in vain; he is the servant of God to execute his wrath on the wrongdoer. Therefore one must be subject, not only to avoid God's wrath but also for the sake of conscience. For the same reason you also pay taxes, for the authorities are ministers of God, attending to this very thing. Pay all of them their dues, taxes to whom taxes are due, revenue to whom revenue is due, respect to whom respect is due, honor to whom honor is due.

Owe no one anything, except to love one another; for he who loves his neighbor has fulfilled the law. The commandments, "You shall not commit adultery, You shall not kill, You shall not steal, You shall not covet," and any other commandment, are summed up in this sentence, "You shall love your neighbor as yourself." Love does no wrong to a neighbor; therefore love is the fulfilling of the law.

—Romans 13:1–10

13

The Moral Minority

In this text, Paul deals with an issue that is being discussed once again in American life, the issue between religion and politics, church and state. It is a difficult passage for us because it is written as specific advice to a particular congregation living two thousand years ago in a culture radically different from ours.

Rome in the first century was not America in the twentieth. Rome was a political tyranny and America is a representative democracy. The church in Rome was made up of people who had no political influence or voice. The church in America could be a formidable political power, if it ever wanted to be, not just because of its numbers but because its members are in high places. In the last presidential election, all three major candidates publicly confessed their Christianity. First-century Rome was never like that.

If Paul had written a letter to the Americans in the latter part of the twentieth century, he might have given different advice than he gave the Romans in the first century. But it is to the Romans that he wrote the message of this chapter so his counsel needs to be interpreted for our time.

The first principle Paul sets forth is the necessity of government. He writes, "There is no government anywhere that God has not placed in power" (Rom. 13:1, TLB). That is Paul's way of saying that government is a necessity. The function of government is to provide an orderly environment for human life. Church and state relationships were not a major concern of Paul's writing so we only have a hint of a doctrine. It will not be until later, after the church is a large established institution and the state begins to emerge as a rival power, that the issue will be dealt with systematically. Luther was one of the first to do so and he used this "hint" in Romans as the starting point of the doctrine he called "The Orders of Creation." Luther's exposition enables us to get at what Paul means.

Luther said that after God created the world he looked upon it all and said, "It is good." There was peace among all people and harmony between human life and the rest of creation. That is the way the world should be, that is the way God created it to be, and that is the way it will be again someday.

But in the meantime human sin has just about ruined the place. The consequence of sin is that the intended peace and harmony have been replaced by discord and strife. God, in his mercy, according to Luther, responded by ordaining certain human institutions with the responsibility of preserving the goodness of life. That is what Paul means when he writes that the rulers are instituted by God.

In the Middle Ages, these institutions were called "estates," and there were three of them: royalty, the church, and the commons or the knights. All three had a responsibility to society and to God to preserve the goodness of life.

It is significant that Luther called marriage an estate, and to this day in the United Methodist ritual, marriage is defined as "an honorable estate, instituted of God," and "therefore not to be entered into unadvisedly, but reverently, discreetly, and in the fear of God." Because the dominant ethic in our day is the fulfillment of one's own self and one's own desires, it is very difficult to get young people seeking marriage in the church to understand that they are entering a vocation of service. But the church still interprets marriage as a "holy estate instituted of God," an order of creation, into which you enter not only for your own personal fulfillment but to contribute to the order and stability of society through a Christian home.

So when western society was taking shape at the end of the Middle Ages, certain vocations were set aside as having crucial importance for the strength of society. Their function was to preserve the goodness of life. They are still around. We don't call them "holy estates" or "orders of creation" anymore, but if you want to know what they are, ask what vocations you still enter by taking vows. Those are the institutions in our time that society considers critical for the preservation of the goodness of life. They are marriage, law and the courts, the church, and government service. You are to enter all of them reverently, discreetly, and in the fear of God because society and God call you to enter them to contribute to the preservation of the goodness of life.

It is that understanding of the vocation of government that leads Paul to say to the Romans that rulers are instituted of God. Because of the kind of world we live in, the human propensity to sin, government is necessary.

In the play *A Man for All Seasons,* Sir Thomas More is talking to his son-in-law, William Roper, one of those idealists who believe that dismantling the corrupt institutions will rid society of injustice. Roper says that he would cut down every law in England to get at the devil. Thomas More replies:

> Oh? and when the last law was down, and the devil turned on you, where would you hide, the laws all being flat? This country's planted thick with laws from coast to coast, man's laws, not God's—and if you cut them down, d'you really think that you could stand upright in the winds that would blow then?

He is saying that if there were no laws, no institutions, no government, the winds of chaos would so devastate society that human life would be impossible. That is the kind of realism about human nature you find in the Bible, especially in Paul's letters, and why he tells the Romans that government is a necessity ordained by God.

The second point is, government is not God. Christians in Germany during World War II faced a moral dilemma. As Lutherans, they were raised with the catechism's instruction to obey the rulers because they were ordained by God. They were faced with a leader demanding absolute obedience to those who were committing crimes against humanity, and who, therefore, were not a part of the preservation of human life, but part of the chaos.

They turned to the Bible for guidance and found that Paul's is not the only instruction on the relation of Christians to the state. In the Book of Revelation, contrary to Paul, Rome is seen not as ordained by God, but as the instrument of Satan. The teaching of Revelation is that when a ruler, or a state, puts itself in the place of God, it is no longer to be supported. It is to be resisted. The Christians at the end of that first century, the time of the writing of the Book of Revelation, resisted the government and paid the price with martyrdom.

Governments are human creations, ordained by God. They are not God. Our ultimate loyalty belongs to God alone. I take the phrase in the Pledge of Allegiance, "one nation under God," to mean that this nation is not God but stands under the judgment of God.

In Second Samuel we find a description of Nathan the prophet condemning David the king. David has stolen Uriah's wife, Bathsheba, and sent Uriah to the front with orders to be so placed in the battle as to insure his death. Nathan confronts David with a story in which a powerful man takes advantage of a poor man. Nathan asks the King who was the criminal in this story. When David responds that it is the powerful man, Nathan points his finger and says, "You are that man."

Nathan is the first of a line of prophets in the Old Testament to preach that even kings stand under the judgment of God and are accountable for their actions. If God ordains rulers he also calls prophets whose purpose is to remind kings they are not God.

When King Henry VIII was trading in wives as if they were used cars, a new one every year, Martin Luther wrote him a letter of reprimand, "From Martin Luther, minister at Wittenberg by the grace of God, to Henry, king of England by the disgrace of God."

Governments are ordained by God, but governments are not God.

Thirdly, Christians must not assume they are morally superior to other people. There are some Christians today who have recently awakened to the importance of a religious voice in the political debate in a democratic republic. Other Christians have always believed they had a responsibility to contribute to the building of a better world and to the maintaining of the quality of life in their nation, and that the best way of doing that in a democratic society is through political action. Christians ought to participate in politics. That needs to be said.

But they ought to do it with humility. And that needs to be underscored. Christians are not given any political wisdom, or superior righteousness denied others. Christians will make as many dumb decisions as anyone else, and be as blind to their sin and to the way their self-interest determines the decision they make as non-Christians. All we need to do is look at history during those periods when Christians were in power to see that they were neither better nor worse than anybody else, until they said that what they were doing was done in the name of God, and then they were invariably worse.

There are political action groups that assert that the candidates they endorse and the issues they advocate are endorsed by God. To make such a statement is simple arrogance, and the most dangerous kind of politics. In politics it is always dangerous to presume that what you are doing is what God would do. You should have the courage to do what you think you ought to do, and then face the consequences yourself. Don't put the blame on God. And after you have acted out of your own conscience, you ought to pray to God that if what you have done is not what he wanted, there won't be too much damage. Christians have no greater wisdom or righteousness than anyone else. Therefore they ought to participate in politics with humility.

In Stephen Vincent Benet's poem called *John Brown's Body,* he captures Lincoln's impatience with those well-meaning Christians who came to him with word that they knew what God's will for him was. Benet has Lincoln say this:

> They come to me and talk about God's will
> In righteous deputations and platoons,
> Day after day, laymen and ministers.
> They write me Prayers From Twenty Million Souls
> Defining me God's will and Horace Greeley's,
> God's will is General This and Senator That,
> God's will is those poor colored fellows' will,
> It is the will of the Chicago churches,
> It is this man's and his worst enemy's.
> But all of them are sure they know God's will.
> I am the only man who does not know it.
> And, yet, if it is probable that God
> Should, and so very clearly, state His will
> To others, on a point of my own duty,
> It might be thought He would reveal it to me
> Directly, more especially as I
> So earnestly desire to know His will.

Christians should participate in politics, they have something to offer. But they should participate with humility.

The final lesson is that Christianity's most important contribution to any nation is to be a moral minority. The first part of this text says in effect, "Do your duty as citizens." The responsibility of any citizen is to pay the taxes, to obey the rulers. "Do your duty," Paul says. But there is nothing particularly Christian about that advice.

When he gets to the tenth verse, he gets to the real contribution the church can make to the state. It is as if he were saying this is your real mission. This is what you ought to be doing as Romans or as Americans. "Owe no one anything, except to love one another; for he who loves his neighbor has fulfilled the law."

Laws and governments are negative restraints against sin. They should be supported as necessary to preserve the goodness of life. But that is not the end of it for Christians. It is just the beginning.

Christians are called to live their lives in service to other people. They are called to be a positive influence in society, not just to support the negative restraints of society. They are called to make society a more human place for all people. And so far, from what I have been able to see, those who have done that in any age are always a minority.

Laws can't make a society moral. If a society doesn't want to obey the laws, it won't. Our problem is not that we don't have laws sufficient enough to punish immorality, but that we don't have models attractive enough to encourage morality.

A couple of years ago the *Christian Science Monitor* ran a series of articles on morality in American life. At the conclusion they looked back on the contributions that had been made by prominent Americans to that series, and were surprised at the number of people who said that what America needs are moral examples. David Riesman, the socioligist, said that we need moral examples throughout the structures of society, but he centered especially on government. Harold Howe II, the vice president of the Ford Foundation, said that in New York City, ghetto schools that were showing success were schools where the principal presented a high moral example. Kenneth Boulding, economist at the University of Colorado, said, "For any individual, example is terribly important. You don't teach morality. You catch it—like an infection, a good one."

The crisis of morality in our country exists not for lack of laws, but for lack of example in government, in business, in parenting, in teaching, and in the church, the institutions of society entrusted with preserving the goodness of life.

We don't need more laws. We need a moral minority to be a leaven for the renewal of society. That is the mission Paul gave the Romans. Do your duty to the state; pay your taxes and obey the laws. Then get to the more important work, the work God requires of you: "Owe no one anything, except to love your neighbor; for he who loves his neighbor has fulfilled the law" (Rom. 13:8).